A BEGINNER'S GUIDE TO GREEK MYTHOLOGY

An Introduction to the Gods and Goddesses, Mythical Creatures, and Muses of Ancient Greece

Neve Sullivan

Intrepidas Publishing

All rights reserved.

© Copyright 2024 by Neve Sullivan.

All rights reserved.

The content contained within this book may not be reproduced, duplicated or transmitted without direct written permission from the author or the publisher.

Under no circumstances will any blame or legal responsibility be held against the publisher, or author, for any damages, reparation, or monetary loss due to the information contained within this book, either directly or indirectly.

Legal Notice:

This book is copyright-protected. It is only for personal use. You cannot amend, distribute, sell, use, quote or paraphrase any part, or the content within this book, without the consent of the author or publisher.

Disclaimer Notice:

Please note the information contained within this document is for educational and entertainment purposes only. All effort has been executed to present accurate, up-to-date, reliable, complete information. No warranties of any kind are declared or implied. Readers acknowledge that the author is not engaged in the rendering of legal, financial, medical or professional advice. The content within this book has been derived from various sources. Please consult a licensed professional before attempting any techniques outlined in this book.

By reading this document, the reader agrees that under no circumstances is the author responsible for any losses, direct or indirect, that are incurred as a result of the use of the information contained within this document, including, but not limited to, errors, omissions, or inaccuracies.

CONTENTS

Introduction	VII
What Is Greek Mythology?	
1. The Greek Pantheon:	1
Meet the Gods and Goddesses	
Meet the 12 Olympians	
The "Outsider Gods"	
Lesser-Known Deities	
Meet the Women	
Summary	
2. The Heroic Age:	15
Meet the Heroes and Heroines	
Heroes and Heroines of Ancient Greece	
Heroines	
Summary	
3. Love Stories From Olympus:	30
Meet the Lovers	
Divine Romances	
Star-Crossed Lovers: Tragic Romances of Greek Myth	

    Summary

4. Mythical Creatures: 44
   Meet the Beasts
       The Famous Monsters of Greek Myth
       Monstrous Females
       Deeper Meanings: When Concepts Become Creatures
       Summary

5. The Creation Myths: 55
   Origins of the Universe
       The Creation Myth
       The Creation of Humankind
       Summary

6. Death and the Afterlife: 67
   Journeys to the Underworld
       The Underworld Deities
       The Kingdom of Hades: Denizens of the Underworld
       Mortal Journeys to the Underworld
       Cycles of Rebirth and Regeneration in Greek Myth
       Summary

7. Metamorphosis Myths: 79
   Transformations and Shape-Shifting
       Godly Transformations
       Gods Transforming Mortals—Causes and Consequences
       Animal and Plant Metamorphosis Stories
       Other Categories of Transformation
       Summary

8. Mythology of the Mind: 91
   Archetypes and Psychology
      Jungian Archetypes in Greek Mythology
      Freudian Interpretations of Greek Myth:
      Oedipus and Electra
      Lessons About Personal Growth From Greek Mythology
      Summary

9. Mythology Meets Philosophy: 103
   Wisdom of the Ancient Greeks
      Relevance of Myth to Stoicism, Cynicism, and Other Greek
      Philosophical Schools
      Lessons on Life, Love, and Wisdom in Greek Mythology
      Summary

10. Comparative Mythology: 113
    Universal Themes and Motifs
       Similarities and Differences to Roman Mythology and the Etruscan Pantheon
       Other Mythic Parallels
       The Universal Motifs of Mythology
       Summary

11. The Muses' Legacy: 125
    How Greek Mythology Continues to Shape Our World
       Modern Adaptations of Greek Myths
       Greek Mythology in Popular Culture Today: Reinterpretations and Retellings
       Summary

12. Conclusion	133
What We Have Learned	
Other Books	138
About the Author	139
References & Bibliography	141

INTRODUCTION

Orpheus with his lute made trees,
And the mountain tops that freeze,
Bow themselves when he did sing:
To his music plants and flowers
Ever sprung; as sun and showers.

– William Shakespeare,
from "Orpheus With His Lute Made Trees"

G reek mythology is overwhelmingly complex, and it can easily become confusing. On top of that, there's the question of relevance. It's ancient history—why bother to read about it today? First, there are all the gods, and then there are all the myths. Do any of these things have any bearing on modern life? How do you even make sense of it all?

This book seeks to address both questions by providing a broad overview and a simple but detailed exploration of Greek mythology, including its relevance to our modern lives. It aims to help those unfamiliar with the canon understand and unravel what seems like a forbiddingly complicated subject.

What Is Greek Mythology?

Greek mythology comprises more than stories about the lives and activities of deities, heroes, and mythological creatures. It is also the narratives the ancient Greeks told to explain the origin and nature of the world, and it is evidence of the beginnings and significance of their cultural and ritual practices. Greek myth sheds light on ancient Greece's religious and political institutions and helps us better comprehend the nature of mythmaking itself. It is a form of ancient folklore and, alongside Roman myths, forms part of the core of classical mythology.

Our understanding of Greek mythology comes from several separate literary sources. The most prominent of these are the epic poems by Homer (ca. 850–800 B.C.E.), the *Iliad* and the *Odyssey,* and the works of Hesiod, namely *Theogony* and *Works and Days*. Information also comes from archaeological finds such as the remains of temples, pottery, paintings, and statues.

Ancient Greek mythology was spread through an oral-poetic tradition, most likely by Minoan and Mycenaen singers, starting in the 18th century B.C.E. (Cartwright, 2012a). Some scholars have proposed that the myths were informed by the Mycenaean religion, as this pantheon of gods includes many deities found in classical Greek myth. An alternative proposal is that they were influenced by pre-Greek or Near Eastern cultures and were thus a successor to an even more ancient Proto-Indo-European religion (Puhvel, 1987).

The Enduring Influence of Greek Mythology

This body of legends is worth learning about because it remains relevant today due to its exploration of universal human experiences, emotions, and problems. Examples include Icarus's attempts to fly too close to the sun or the consequences of Narcissus's fascination with his appearance. It also contains moral, ethical, and philosophical lessons. Referring to one of the examples above, Icarus's story teaches us that if we seek out danger or get carried away by ambition, we will inevitably fall, fail, or get found out.

Greek mythology has also had a profound influence on modern culture. It has informed Western literature, art, philosophy, and even psychology—as demonstrated by the concept of the Oedipus complex. This is the term Sigmund Freud introduced that has come to refer to the feelings or attitude of young men who are fascinated by much older women, or even their mothers—as the hero after which it was named famously and unwittingly married his.

Although myths can be hard to make sense of, they often contain hidden meanings of a timeless nature, which remain relevant. Together with legends, they are cultural reflections, and there is no right or wrong way to interpret them.

Many of these tales have been adapted countless times across different cultures, languages, and media over the centuries. They remain part of the Western language and heritage. Poets from ancient times to the present day have been inspired by its characters and their stories and have rediscovered the significance and relevance of its themes in different times and contexts.

A Quick Primer

Greek mythology offers a rich mixture of tales, many of which have influenced our culture and thought. However, myths aren't just stories: They are intricate narratives that reflect the beliefs, values, and cultures of ancient societies.

The pantheon of Greek deities is large, with each god or goddess having their own domain and responsibilities. Each of them also had several symbols associated with them, for example, Zeus's thunderbolt and Athena's owl. Additionally, Poseidon's trident and Hermes's winged sandals show how certain objects became iconic because of their association with a specific deity.

The creation myth of Greek mythology, too, is complex and involves the birth and overthrow of several generations of gods until Zeus takes control.

Gods were not infallible in Greek mythology—they had flaws such as Hera's jealousy or Zeus's wrath, that make them relatable to humans. There are also heroes like Heracles, known for his superhuman strength, and Achilles, whose only vulnerability as a warrior was his heel. These figures often found themselves in adventures involving quests or tasks set by others—usually gods—that tested their mettle in various ways.

Other characters or tropes that frequently appear are oracles, who played a significant role by providing prophecies about future events which often shaped characters' decisions. Meanwhile, monsters like Medusa or the Cyclopes were used to personify certain fears or societal evils.

Myths also explored themes like fate versus free will, as in the tale of Oedipus, or hubris leading to downfall, as with Icarus. The Trojan War is one of the most famous stories from Greek mythology. Other than telling of cunning strategies like the Trojan Horse, it also highlights themes like love through the characters of Paris and Helen and pride, as exemplified by Achilles.

Myths were an integral part of religious rites and ceremonies in ancient Greece. Thus, they reflected deep-seated cultural beliefs, such as in divine intervention and natural phenomena occurring through the actions of the gods. Furthermore, most cities had a patron deity that they revered and celebrated with special festivals and rituals.

Myths have also evolved and transformed over time. This was partly because they were transmitted orally, which gave the teller the freedom to adjust the narrative to fit a specific purpose. Also, ancient Greek myth informed its Roman counterpart, meaning it was ultimately transformed to meet the needs of a different classical society.

So, if you want to better understand the significance of Greek mythology and its continued impact, read on...

Chapter 1

The Greek Pantheon:

Meet the Gods and Goddesses

Even the sun
Whose light
Rules all the
Stars has known
Love's kingdom.

–Ovid, from "Aphrodite"

The people of ancient Greece believed that their gods and goddesses watched over them and that, from time to time, they would interfere with the events on Earth. The deities could send storms if they were angry and decide which side would win in war...

Because of the significance of these figures, in this chapter, we make sense of the pantheon and become familiar with the major and lesser-known gods and goddesses. Although the core group of Greek gods is made up of the 12 Olympians who lived on top of Mount Olympus, the ancient Greeks also worshipped many local and lesser deities. We will thus explore as many of these figures as possible and discuss their role in myths.

Meet the 12 Olympians

Greek myth tells us that the 12 Olympians came to power after defeating the Titans, led by their parents, Cronus and Rhea, in the War of the Titans, also known as the Titanomachy. The dozen principal gods and goddesses (apart from Hades, the ruler of the underworld) lived on Mount Olympus, where the weather was always spring-like, and a ring of ice separated the inhabitants from the mortals who lived below.

While the Olympians were the most powerful and significant deities in Greek myth, they were depicted as having the same desires, inclinations, flaws, and strengths as mortals. Sometimes, they were even described as living in similar conditions. Although they looked like humans, they were generally prettier and stronger than their earthly counterparts; they could also transform at will and teleport anywhere they wanted to go.

Zeus: King of the Gods and Ruler of the Skies

Zeus was the king of the Olympians, the ruler of Mount Olympus, and the god of the sky, thunder, lightning, law, order, and justice. He was the youngest child of Cronus and Rhea, the brother and husband of Hera, and also a sibling of Poseidon, Hades, Demeter, and Hestia.

Zeus was also known for his many affairs with goddesses and mortals alike. Some examples are those he had with Demeter, his sister, and Leto, one of the Titans, as well as the mortals Leda and Alcmene (Hamilton, 2017).

His symbols include the eagle, the thunderbolt, the oak tree, the scepter, and scales.

Hera: Goddess of Marriage and Monogamy

As the wife of the king of the gods, Hera was their queen. She was also the goddess of women, childbirth, and family. She was the youngest daughter of Cronus and Rhea, making her Zeus's sister as well as his spouse.

Her husband was often unfaithful and had many extramarital affairs. In contrast, as marriage was another of her domains, Hera wanted a monogamous partnership and often tried to get revenge on his lovers and their children.

Her symbols are the peacock, the cow, and the cuckoo.

Poseidon: God of the Seas, Earthquakes, and Horses

Poseidon was the middle son of Cronus and Rhea, so he was older than Zeus but younger than Hades. While he was married to the Nereid nymph, Amphitrite, like his brother and many other Greek gods, he also had many lovers. Poseidon was the god of the seas, storms, water, earthquakes, hurricanes, and horses.

His symbols include the dolphin, the trident, and the bull.

Demeter: Goddess of the Harvest

Demeter was the middle daughter of Cronus and Rhea and the lover of Zeus and Poseidon, her brothers. Her children were Persephone, Arion, and Despoine. As the goddess of the harvest, agriculture, fertility, nature, and the seasons, her role was to preside over the grains and prosperity of the earth.

Demeter's symbols are wheat and the poppy, the torch, the pig, and the cornucopia.

Athena: Goddess of Wisdom, War, and Crafts

Athena was the daughter of Zeus and the Oceanid nymph, Metis. Her birth was memorable, as she rose from her father's head as a grown woman in full battle armor. She was the goddess of wisdom, warfare, and handicrafts.

Athena's symbols include the olive tree and the owl.

Apollo: God of the Sun, Music, and Prophecy

Apollo was the son of Zeus and Leto, and he was the twin brother of Artemis. He was the god of the sun, light, philosophy, prophecy, truth, archery, inspiration, poetry, the arts, music, medicine, manly beauty, healing, and plague.

Apollo's symbols are the bow and arrow, the raven, the lyre, the swan, and the wolf.

Artemis: Goddess of the Hunt and the Moon

Artemis was the twin of Apollo. She was the goddess of the hunt, virginity, the wilderness, the moon, childbirth, and protection. Similarly to her brother, she was also the goddess of archery and plague.

Artemis has several symbols, including the deer, the horse, the hound, the she-bear, the snake, the cypress tree, and the moon. She also shares the bow and arrow with Apollo.

Ares: God of War and Bloodlust

Ares, the son of Zeus and Hera, was hated by all the other gods apart from Aphrodite. He was unpopular because, as the god of war, violence, manly virtue, and bloodshed, he represented the distasteful aspects of brutal battle and slaughter.

Ares's symbols are the boar, the dog, the serpent, the vulture, the shield, and the spear.

Aphrodite: Goddess of Love and Beauty

According to Homer, Aphrodite was the daughter of Zeus and the Titaness and Oceanid, or Titanide, Dione. In Hesiod's account, however, she was born from sea foam. After the Titan Cronus castrated his father, Uranus, he threw the severed genitals into the sea. The goddess of love was then conceived from the droplets of blood that had dripped into the water. She was married to Hephaestus, but, like many of her fellow gods, she had many affairs, most notably with Ares.

Aphrodite's symbols include the bird, the dove, the bee, the apple, the myrtle, the swan, and the rose.

Hephaestus: God of Fire and Metalworking

Hephaestus was the son of Hera and was either sired by Zeus or conceived through parthenogenesis and so fatherless. In the second case, Hera is said to have conceived and given birth to the god of metalwork alone as a reaction to Athena being born from Zeus's head (Park, 2024). He was married to Aphrodite and was the master blacksmith and craftsman to the gods. For this reason, his domains were the forge, invention, craftsmanship, fire, and volcanoes.

Hephaestus's symbols are the anvil, the axe, the donkey, the hammer, the quail, fire, and tongs.

Hermes: Messenger of the Gods

Hermes was the son of Zeus and Maia, a Pleiades nymph. He was the second-youngest Olympian, being only slightly older than Dionysus. He was the messenger to the gods and ruled over travel, communication, commerce, borders, diplomacy, eloquence, games, and thieves. He was also a guide to dead souls.

Hermes's symbols include the winged sandals and cap, the stork, the caduceus (a staff entwined with two snakes and a symbol of modern medicine), and the tortoise—the shell of which he used to invent the lyre.

Dionysus: God of Wine and Revelry

Dionysus was the son of Zeus and the mortal Theban princess, Semele, and he was married to the Cretan princess Ariadne. He was the youngest Olympian god and the only one to have a mortal parent. He was also a later addition to the Olympians, as he was originally a demigod before being promoted.

He was the god of wine, fertility, the grapevine, festivity, ecstasy, resurrection, and madness. He was also the patron god of the theater.

Dionysus's symbols include ivy, the grapevine, the tiger, the cup, the panther, the dolphin, the leopard, the pinecone, and the goat.

The "Outsider Gods"

The outsider gods were accepted on Mount Olympus but either did not live there or were not Olympians but still part of the core group of Greek deities.

Hades

Hades was the eldest son of Cronus and Rhea, which meant he was the last son to be regurgitated by his father.

After defeating Cronus and his race of gods, the Titans, Hades, along with his brothers, Zeus and Poseidon, claimed joint rulership of the cosmos. He received the underworld, so he was the god of the dead and reigned over this realm as king. Poseidon took ownership of the sea, and Zeus the sky. Earth (previously the province of Gaia) was available to all three equally.

In art, Hades is depicted as holding a bident and wearing his helm; Cerberus, the three-headed dog that guards his domain, is often standing by his side.

Hecate

Hecate was the daughter of Perses and Asteria, the twin sister of Leto. She was one of the third generation of Titans but sided with the Olympians during Titanomachy. For this reason, Zeus rewarded and honored her by allowing her to operate on Earth, in the sky, and in the underworld.

In the Greek religion, she was the goddess of crossroads, magic, witchcraft, ghosts, sorcery, and necromancy.

Hestia

Hestia was the first child of Cronus and Rhea, making her the elder sister of Hades, Demeter, Poseidon, Hera, and Zeus. She was one of the three virgin goddesses, as she never married nor had children. Although Poseidon and Apollo asked for her hand in marriage, she refused them both. She was the goddess of the hearth, fire, family order, and domesticity.

Although she does not feature in the list of the 12 gods above, some others include Hestia instead of Dionysus, as she was one of the original Olympians. One story has it that because she was content to tend to her hearth in Olympus, she gave up her throne for the god of wine (Fatica,

2021). However, this account appears to be a modern invention and to have originated with the poet, author, and classical scholar Robert Graves.

Lesser-Known Deities

Many people believe that the 12 Olympians listed above are the only Greek deities. This is far from true. There were 3,142 Greek gods and goddesses in total, and every city in Greece had a patron god or goddess who citizens believed protected them from harm. Some of these figures are extremely obscure, and we only know their name and parentage.

Nemesis

Hesiod refers to Nemesis, telling us that she was one of the children of Nyx—the daughter of Chaos and goddess of the night. Different sources say that her father was Oceanus, Erebus, or Zeus. She is also said to be the mother of Helen of Troy and the four Telchines, sea magicians and inventors of metalwork, by Tartarus.

Also called Rhamnousia, as in "the goddess of Rhamnous," an ancient city in Attica, she personified and enacted personal retribution for the sin of hubris (exaggerated pride or self-confidence) or arrogance before the gods.

Iris

Iris was the daughter of the gods Thaumas and Electra, and Hesiod says that she was sister to the Harpies Arke and Ocypete. She was the personification of the rainbow and served as a messenger of the gods and servant to the Olympians, particularly Hera.

In several stories Iris appears, carrying messages to and from the gods and running errands for them; however, she has no unique mythology of her own, and little evidence of her worship in the ancient world survives.

Helios

Helios was the god of the sun and a minor deity in classical Greece. His parents were Hyperion and Theia, the latter of whom was also referred to as Euryphaessa, Aethra, or Basileia. He was the only brother of the goddesses Eos and Selene. Although he was only a minor god, his origin is ancient, so the other deities avoided meddling with him (Ogden, 2001).

The Primordial Pantheon

Greek mythology begins at the start of the world. In *Theogony*, Hesiod presents a complete cosmology that describes how natural forces were personified and how these deities served as the most basic parts of the cosmos. As such, they did not possess human characteristics, as the later gods did; rather they were representations of concepts or places.

The primordial pantheon were the parents to the successive generations, and the Titans were the children of some of the first gods, namely Gaia and Uranus. Six of them were male and six were female, namely: Cronus, Oceanus, Coeus, Hyperion, Iapetus, Crius, Rhea, Tethys, Theia, Phoebe, Themis, and Mnemosyne.

Two other species were also the offspring of Gaia and Uranus. These were the monstrous Hecatoncheires, or the "hundred-handed ones" and the Cyclopes, meaning "circle-eyed" or "one-eyed." (You will read more about these beasts and others in Chapter 4.)

After Uranus mistreated the Hecatoncheires and the Cyclopes, Gaia ordered the Titans to overthrow their father, leading to them becoming the main gods before the Olympians took over.

As mentioned above, Cronus and Rhea were the parents of the 12 Olympians and heads of the Titans. Cronus was keen to hold onto his power, so he ate each one of his children whole after they were born, apart from Zeus. In his case, as his mother presented her husband with a rock dressed in swaddling clothes to prevent her youngest child from sharing the same fate. Eventually, the surviving child rose against the leader of the Titans, and he forced him to regurgitate his siblings, after which they banded together to overthrow their father (Kapach, 2023).

Meet the Women

The Greek pantheon includes numerous goddesses; however, they shared in the oppression their mortal counterparts experienced. In classical society, women were subservient to men and had little freedom. Despite their immortality and strength, the Greek goddesses were often similarly subject to the whims and desires of the gods or were banned from wielding power in their own right.

Examples include Aphrodite, the goddess of love, who was, ironically, trapped in a loveless marriage; Hera, the goddess of marriage, who was wed to a man who constantly had affairs; and Athena, the wisest of beings, who had to defer to Zeus and Hera in everything.

Despite this bleak picture, several separate categories of female Greek goddesses had their individual, unique functions. These include the Horae and ideal feminine archetypes such as the nymphs, the Muses, and the Graces.

The Horae: Goddesses of the Seasons

The Horae were the goddesses of the seasons and the natural passing of time. Their name comes from the word "hora" which has its origins in the Proto-Indo-European word for "year," which is also said to mean "the correct moment" (Kerenyi, 1951: 101).

Originally, they were the personifications of nature in its different phases. Later on, they were seen as goddesses of order and natural justice. To this end, they came and went, bringing and bestowing ripeness according to the laws of the earth and life. They also guarded the gates of Olympus, railed the stars and constellations, and promoted the earth's fertility.

Nymphs

In Greek mythology, the word "nymph" is used to describe a large class of inferior female divinities. These creatures were associated with fertility and growth (such as of trees) and water. They were not immortal, but they had extremely long lifespans, and they were generally kindly toward men.

The nymphs were categorized according to the area of nature they were connected to. Some of these include:

- **The Oceanids:** Sea nymphs.

- **The Nereids:** Lived in both saltwater and freshwater.

- **The Naiads:** Presided over rivers, springs, and lakes.

- **The Oreads:** Were the nymphs of mountains and grottos.

- **The Napaeae ("dell") and the Alseids ("grove"):** The nymphs of glens and groves.

- **The Dryads or Hamadryads:** The nymphs of the forests and trees.

The Muses: Patrons of the Arts and Sciences

The Muses were the goddesses that inspired literature, the arts, and science. The ancient Greeks believed them to be the source of the knowledge that's found in the poetry, myths, and lyrics of songs that humans recited orally for centuries and formed the foundation of culture.

The name and number of the Muses differed by region. However, from the classical period onward, the number has been fixed at nine (Grimal, 1996). Their names are usually given as Calliope, Polyhymnia, Clio, Euterpe, Erato, Terpsichore, Melpomene, Urania, and Thalia.

The Graces: Goddesses of Charm, Beauty, and Creativity

The Graces, also known as the Charities, were sister goddesses of beauty, fertility, and charm. Their names are Aglaea (meaning "radiance" or "beauty"), Euphrosyne (meaning "joy"), and Thalia (meaning "bloom"). A fourth Grace, Peitho, representing persuasion, was later introduced in the writings of the poet Hermesianax.

In Greek mythology, the group of goddesses represented the divine incarnation of the qualities of grace and beauty as well as acts of charity through gift-giving, reciprocity, and generosity

Summary

There are so many Greek gods and goddesses that it is impossible to cover them all here, but we hope we have introduced you to the flavor of these personalities and the mythological system they were a part of. They also had huge significance for the ancient Greek worldview. Citizens made offerings to appease them, and they believed that the deities had power over the elements, which would affect the harvest. In this sense, they believed that worshipping the gods and goddesses was essential for the survival of their civilization.

In this next chapter, we move along to look at the stories of the heroes and heroines of Greek myth.

Chapter 2
The Heroic Age:
Meet the Heroes and Heroines

Sing, goddess, the anger of Peleus' son Achilleus
and its devastation, which put pains thousandfold upon the
Achaians,
hurled in their multitudes to the house of Hades strong souls
of heroes, but gave their bodies to be the delicate feasting
of dogs, of all birds, and the will of Zeus will be accomplished.
— Homer, from "The Iliad"

As the Greeks loved to share stories about brave heroes and their great adventures, in this chapter, we look at the accounts of these men as well as those of the heroines and human champions that feature throughout Greek mythology.

In modern usage, the word "hero" has positive connotations and describes someone who accomplishes great feats and inspires admiration and emulation. However, for the Greeks, a hero did not have to be moral; he or she just had to be brave. Some engaged in deeds of great valor while others are known only for having killed in extraordinary circumstances.

What unites Greek heroes is that they were all mortals, not gods. All of them lived and died either in the remote past or more ancient times. Having said that, it is also important to mention that these legendary characters were usually the children of a god and a mortal, which meant that they were stronger and more courageous than ordinary people.

Below, we continue the Greek tradition by sharing some of the stories of their heroes.

Heroes and Heroines of Ancient Greece

Here, we look at some of the best-known stories of heroes and heroines found in Greek mythology.

The 12 Labors of Heracles: From Zero to Hero to God

One of the Greek tradition's favorite heroes was Heracles (called Hercules by the Romans). He was the mortal son of Zeus and was so strong that he could kill a lion with his bare hands. Like many of his counterparts, he was flawed. He was brave and strong but also had an uncontrollable temper.

Heracles demonstrated god-like strength at an early age. Zeus's wife, Hera, was jealous of the affair between her husband and the hero's mother, Alcmene. When he was an infant, Hera reacted by putting two giant snakes in his crib, hoping that they would crush him to death. Instead, the child used his superhuman strength and strangled the serpents.

As an adult, Heracles performed many great feats and went on many adventures, including sailing with Jason and the Argonauts to find the Golden Fleece and performing 12 "impossible" tasks. The latter are perhaps his most famous deeds. These labors were set for him by Eurystheus, king of Tiryns, as penance for the hero killing his wife and children (Wilkinson, 1998). In order, these labors were:

1. **Nemean Lion:** A lion that had a skin so tough that no weapon could pierce it lived at Nemea. To defeat it, Heracles made a massive club, beat the creature, and strangled it. Using the beast's sharp claws, he then removed its hide and wore it to protect himself.

2. **Lernean Hydra:** The Hydra, a nine-headed dragon, dwelled in the lake of Lerna. When one of its heads was cut off, two more would grow in its place. Heracles defeated the monster with the help of his nephew, Iolaus. The two worked as a team, with the young man burning each neck as soon as the hero cut off one of the heads to prevent any new growths.

3. **Ceryneian Hind:** Heracles had to capture the hind with golden horns that lived on top of Mount Ceryneia without harming it, as it was sacred to the goddess Artemis. After he'd chased the beast for a year, he finally captured it in a net. But the deer was wounded in the struggle, and Heracles blamed Eurystheus for its wounds so that Artemis would not be angry with him.

4. **Erymanthian Boar:** This was a giant creature that terrorized the people who lived around Mount Erymanthus. Heracles was asked

to bring the boar back alive to Eurystheus, who was so scared of the beast that he kept it in an urn.

5. **Augean Stables:** Augeas, the king of Elis, had filthy stables that had never been tended to. As a result, dung had been accumulating for years. Heracles, tasked with cleaning the mess in one day, diverted two rivers to wash the filth away.

6. **Stymphalian Birds:** The people of Lake Stymphalos were being preyed on by man-eating birds. So, to rid them of their tormentors, Heracles scared the creatures out of the trees and shot them with his arrows as they took flight.

7. **Cretan Bull:** A fire-breathing bull—also the father of the famous beast known as the Minotaur—was rampaging across the island of Crete. Heracles was tasked with capturing it alive and taking it back to Tiryns.

8. **Mares of Diomedes:** The despotic Thracian king, Diomedes, fed human flesh to his mares. To complete this task, Heracles killed the king and fed him to the horses, which he then tamed and took to the Tiryns.

9. **Girdle of Hippolyte:** Eurystheus wanted a beautiful girdle that belonged to Hippolyte, an Amazonian queen. After fighting and killing her, Heracles took her belt.

10. **Cattle of Geryon:** The three-bodied monster Geryon kept a herd of red cattle. Heracles killed him and his giant herdsman before

capturing the creatures.

11. **Apples of the Hesperides:** The Hesperides, a group of nymphs, kept a tree that had golden apples, which was also guarded by Ladon, a dragon. To complete this task, Heracles had to slay the monster to get the fruit.

12. **Cerberus:** Heracles's final task was to capture Cerberus, the three-headed dog that guarded the entrance to the underworld, and take it to the Tiryns.

These labors demonstrate the range of tasks that counted as heroic to the Greeks and the fact that morality did not play a part in their conception of a hero.

As noted above, Heracles was the son of Zeus and a human woman, so he was part god, part mortal. In addition to the labors, Heracles was also famous for being the only human to be given immortality after the mortal side of him died.

This occurred after the hero was tricked into putting on a robe that his lover, Deianira, had dipped in the blood of a centaur combined with the venom of the Hydra. She was so distraught that she hanged herself. As for Heracles, after realizing that he was dying, he resolved to hasten his death. He ordered his son to help him up Mount Oeta, where he built his funeral pyre. A passing shepherd, Philoctetes, lit this, as none of the hero's companions could bring themselves to do it. Only the mortal side of Heracles died in the fire, with Zeus lifting the divine side of him to Mount Olympus.

The Trojan War

The saga of the Trojan War, as told by Homer in his epic, the *Iliad*, tells us about many of the heroes of Greek mythology. Paris, Prince of Troy, fell in love with Helen, the beautiful wife of King Menelaus of Sparta. With the help of Aphrodite, the Trojan royal stole her and took her as his wife. In retaliation, King Menelaus declared war on Troy, beginning a 10-year conflict.

The Greeks were led by Agamemnon, the brother of Menelaus and king of Argos, and the Trojans by the hero Hector. The gods, who took different sides, were also involved. Below, we touch on some of the stories of the many Greek heroes who participated in the war.

Achilles

Achilles was the greatest Greek warrior. He had been dipped into the River Styx as a child so that his whole body, except for his heel, could not be hurt. This made him almost superhuman.

During the Trojan War, he pulled out of the conflict in protest when Agamemnon claimed his war booty. His companion, Patroclus, then put on his armor to make the enemy think that the feared warrior had returned to the fight. A battle followed, and Patroclus was killed. In despair, the real Achilles rejoined the action, in which he killed Hector, the Trojan war hero who had slain his friend. Following this, Paris fatally shot the Greek hero in the heel.

Hector

Hector was the leader of the Trojans and their best warrior. He killed many Greeks, wounded heroes such as Agamemnon and Odysseus, and slew Achilles's close friend, Patroclus. When Achilles learned of the latter's death, he challenged Hector to single combat. Hector hoped to tire Achilles by running around the walls of Troy three times. But the young Greek caught Hector, killed him, and in triumph, dragged his body thrice around the walls behind his chariot.

The Trojan Horse

Perhaps the most famous incident of the war involved the Trojan Horse. This strategy serves as an example of heroic ingenuity and was the brainchild of Odysseus.

The Greeks made a hollow wooden horse, to be occupied by 50 of their warriors, and left it outside the walls of Troy. The Trojans then took it into the city, thinking that it was a peace offering and that their enemy had gone home. At nightfall, the hidden soldiers escaped and opened the gates so that the rest of their army could enter and defeat the Trojans by sacking and destroying the city.

Theseus: The Hero of Athens

Theseus was the son of Aegeus, king of Athens, and is remembered for his many heroic deeds. He slew the Minotaur, the monster that lived on Crete, fought with Heracles against the Amazonians, killed murderers and robbers such as Cercyon and Sciron, defeated the sorceress Medea despite her efforts to kill him, and eventually became king of Athens himself. Some of Theseus's most heroic acts are detailed below.

Theseus and the Minotaur

Every year, King Minos of Crete demanded that seven maidens and seven youths from Athens be fed to the Minotaur, a monster that he kept in a labyrinth near his palace. Theseus traveled from Athens to kill the creature, and, in the process, he was helped by Minos's daughter, Ariadne, on the condition that he take her away from her home.

The princess gave Theseus a thread to unwind so that he could kill the beast and find his way back through the labyrinth afterward. After his success, the lovers escaped by ship. Unfortunately, when they stopped at Naxos, Dionysus, who was in love with Ariadne, cast a spell so that Theseus forgot her and sailed away alone.

Theseus and Sinis

Sinis was the son of the god Poseidon and preyed on unwary travelers. He would stop passersby, torturing and robbing them before tearing them apart between two bent trees. At other times, he would use a bent bine to catapult his victims through the air. Theseus put a stop to this when he killed the bandit by hurling him over a cliff.

Jason and the Argonauts: The Golden Fleece—A Hero's Daunting Quest

Jason was an ancient Greek hero who sailed around the world performing heroic deeds with his companions. Although he was born a prince of Thessaly, he was disinherited by Pelias, his uncle. To keep his nephew away, Pelias sent him on an impossible mission to capture the Golden Fleece.

Jason set sail on his ship, the *Argo*, which had been built by the craftsman Argus. The hero's 50 traveling companions, called the Argonauts, included many Greek heroes such as Heracles. Some of their exciting adventures involved clearing the terrifying giants from the island of Cyzicus, banishing the Harpies from the mouth of the Black Sea, and sailing through the Symplegades, two dangerous moving rocks.

One of the most famous stories about the travelers is their theft of a fleece made of gold that had covered a winged ram named Chrysomallos. When Jason and his companions arrived at Colchis, where it was located, King Aeëtes did not want to part with the treasure, so he gave the hero many impossible tasks to do before he could take it. With the help of magic provided by the sorceress Medea, Aeëtes's daughter, Jason was eventually able to grab his prize and escape (Wilkinson, 1998).

Perseus: Slayer of Monsters

This story tells us how a hero used both bravery and ingenuity to kill a truly fearsome beast.

Perseus boasted that he could behead the Gorgon Medusa, who had the fearsome ability to turn a person to stone with one glance. Realizing that his task would not be easy, he asked the gods for help. Hermes gave the hero his winged sandals, Hades his invisible helmet, and Athena her polished shield.

So equipped, Perseus flew to Medusa's home with the sandals and used the helmet to trick the Graeae, the trio who guarded the three Gorgons. After gaining entry to the cave, he used Athena's shield as a mirror so that he would not have to look directly at Medusa. He then beheaded her with his sword. In his quest, he was assisted by the one eye and tooth shared by the Graeae.

Lesser-Known Heroic Figures

There are many lesser-known heroic figures in the Greek canon. A couple of examples are explored below.

Orpheus: The Legendary Bard

Orpheus was a great musician. He was heartbroken when his wife, the nymph Eurydice, died of a snake bite. To bring her back, he traveled to the underworld and entered by enchanting its guard dog, Cerberus, with his lyre.

Persephone and Hades gave Eurydice permission to follow her husband back to Earth but stipulated that he must not look back at her before leaving the gates. However, the musician could not resist doing this, so she remained in the underworld.

Daedalus: The Masterful Inventor

Daedalus was an artist, craftsman, and inventor who was hired by King Minos to build the labyrinth that housed the Minotaur, which was eventually killed by Theseus. The king was so angry when the hero killed the monster that he imprisoned the inventor and his son, Icarus.

Using his skills, Daedalus planned an ingenious escape by making wings for himself and Icarus, which they attached to themselves with wax. The men then used the contraption to fly away from the island. While his father eventually landed safely, Icarus ignored the warning not to fly too close to the sun. Because of this, the heat melted the wax, and he plunged to his death.

Heroines

It wasn't just men who could be heroes: Women could perform such deeds, too. We look at some examples below.

Atalanta: The Swift-Footed Huntress

Atalanta was something of a trailblazer for women in myth, and there were two versions of the huntress. In one, she was the daughter of Iasus and Clymene and came from Arcadia. In this account, she is known for the tales of the Calydonian boar hunt and was one of Jason's Argonauts. In the second, she came from Boeotia and was the daughter of King Schoeneus, and she was famed for her skill in the footrace. In both versions, Atalanta was allied with Artemis, the goddess of the hunt (Boardman, 1983).

At birth, the Arcadian Atalanta's father left her exposed on Mount Parthenion because he had wanted a son. There, a she-bear—one of the symbols of Artemis—whose cubs had recently been killed by hunters discovered her. The bear nursed her until the same hunters came across the girl and raised her in the mountains themselves. She grew up to be a virgin who rejected all proposals of marriage and devoted herself to the goddess Artemis.

Later, Atalanta sailed with the Argonauts in their quest for the Golden Fleece. However, frustratingly, Jason prevented her from joining the action because he was worried that a woman's presence would cause conflict between the men (Kinsey, 2012).

However, the huntress played a more important role in the Calydonian boar hunt, which stemmed from King Oeneus of Calydon failing to offer any sacrifice to Artemis, who retaliated by sending a wild boar to ravage his kingdom. His son, Meleager, gathered a band of heroes, including Atalanta, to capture and kill it. When they finally caught up with the beast, the heroine wounded it.

Although the injury she inflicted did not kill the beast, it made it easier for others to finish the deed, and Meleager awarded the prize of the boar's skin to Atalanta. This angered the other hunters, especially the prince's uncles Plexippus and Toxeus, as they did not believe a woman should receive such an honor. In retaliation, Meleager killed the men. This act proved to be the prince's undoing, as the Fates had cursed him at birth to only live as long as a certain log remained intact. When his mother, Althaea, heard of the death of her brothers, she was so angry that she took the piece of wood and threw it into the fire, causing her son to die.

While Atalanta was a heroine in her own right, it is unfortunate that her story is eclipsed by the lives and deeds of the men involved in her brave acts.

Penelope

Penelope was not known for her bravery, nor did she perform fearsome deeds. Rather, her heroism was a matter of her devotion to her husband Odysseus, one of the many heroes of the Trojan War, and also her refusal to be married to another man.

She waited faithfully for her husband to return from war and refused to believe he was dead, even though he had been away for a long time. Many suitors tried to persuade her to stop waiting for him and remarry. In response, she told them that she would only do so when she finished work on the tapestry she was weaving. She turned this into an endless task as, each night, she would undo the work she had done during the day. In this way, she was able to keep the men at bay until Odysseus eventually returned.

Her example is yet another that proves how integral the trait of ingenuity was to Greek heroes and heroines. Penelope's story also shows how, in Greek mythology, women were generally given a more passive form of heroism, such as loyalty and endurance, instead of actively leading battle charges. This reflects the status of mortal Greek women, whose activities were limited to the domestic sphere. Nevertheless, these figures were much respected in their own right.

Andromache

The heroism of Andromache, on the other hand, lay in her ability to endure much suffering. She was the wife of Hector, the Trojan military commander and hero. During the war, she was raped, enslaved, and forced to hand over her baby to the Greeks, who then threw him over the city battlements. Despite all of this hardship, Andromache was admired for how she bore her suffering with dignity. After the war, she finally found peace and contentment as the wife of Helenus, king of Epirus.

Pandora

Pandora was the first woman. Under Zeus's orders, she was made out of clay by Hephaestus, the god of fire and metalworking, in retaliation for Prometheus's theft of fire for human use. She was then sent to Earth with a box and was subsequently married to Epimetheus, twin to the fire thief. Eventually, Pandora became curious about what was inside of the box, so she lifted the lid. When she did, all the ills of humankind escaped. By the time she managed to shut it again, all that was left inside was hope.

Because she dared to investigate the unknown, Pandora's story is heroic, despite the awful consequences of her actions. Her example is also demonstrative of the danger female curiosity posed, as this was a threat to the male hierarchy of power. If a woman insisted on seeing clearly and fully understanding the reasons behind her subjugation, there was a risk that she and others might start resisting. This would topple and overthrow the balance of power. Thus, Pandora's example was used to justify the silencing of women for generations to come.

Summary

These stories of heroes and heroines demonstrate how the ancient Greeks valued bravery above all else. They also tell us that heroes often needed to display ingenuity as well as courage and brute force to be victorious. Some examples of this in the canon are Daedalus and his wings and Odysseus and the Trojan Horse. Even Orpheus demonstrated this quality in playing the lyre to enchant Cerberus in his attempt to bring Eurydice back to the world of the living.

In the next chapter, we explore another key theme in Greek myth: Love.

Chapter 3
Love Stories from Olympus:
Meet the Lovers

The mistress of love is not kind
She is not malevolent either. □

–Ovid, from "Aphrodite"

The ancient Greeks are famous for their timeless stories of the power of love and romance.

For the Greeks, love was an integral force. Immediately after Chaos came into being at the beginning of the world, Eros, the god of procreation and desire, followed. His creation at such an early point shows how the ancient Greeks considered love to be one of the world's most vital and necessary powers.

The people of this ancient civilization acknowledged that love and lust are integral parts of the human experience, and this knowledge shaped their myths and religion. The ancient Greeks believed that two kinds of love existed: agape and eros. The latter is erotic and requires mutual feelings of affection to be fully recognized; meanwhile, the former is unselfish and does not need the other party to feel the same way. Both forms were recognized and valued.

Because of the centrality of this theme in ancient Greek culture, they passed down many stories featuring tragically doomed couples, forbidden lovers, and jealous gods, which inspired future generations of poets, painters, playwrights, and sculptors. We explore a few of these tales below.

Divine Romances

Many of the romances in Greek myth feature the gods in leading roles and usually involve their relationships with other mythical creatures or mortals. A small sample can be found below.

The Many Loves of Zeus: Seductions of a Supreme God

Zeus, king of the gods, is famous for his many infidelities. His eye for the ladies was one of his defining characteristics, and he had numerous liaisons with women both before and after his marriage. Hesiod tells us that before marrying Hera, Zeus had relationships with several of the female Titans as well as his sister Demeter. The poet says that the romances occurred in the following order: Metis, Themis, Eurynome, Demeter, Mnemosyne, and finally, Leto. Other authors include Dione, a Titaness, and Persephone in the list of the lovers he took before his marriage. The god also unsuccessfully tried seducing Asteria, the sister of Leto and the mother of Hecate.

While Zeus was married, he had numerous affairs with divine and human women. These affairs significantly impacted his dynamic with Hera, and their relationship was often strained as a result. The infidelities with mortals were particularly distressing to his wife, as they threatened the sanctity of their marriage and Hera's position as queen of the gods.

The Olympian queen was known to be vindictive and act on her jealous nature. She often sought revenge against her husband's lovers. Some notable examples are her transformation of Callisto into a bear and the time she sent a serpent to kill Leto and the twins she had conceived with Zeus.

As you can see, Zeus's infidelities were numerous and varied, but they all share a common theme: His lust for women. We retell some of these stories below.

Europa

Europa was a mortal princess from the ancient Phoenician city of Tyre. Like many of Zeus's lovers, she was renowned for her beauty and being an ideal example of ancient Greek womanhood.

The king of the gods was determined to seduce her, so he transformed into a white bull to lure her away from her friends while she and her companions were picking flowers and walking along a beach. The girls soon noticed the beast due to his beauty and docile behavior and went over to pet him. Europa then climbed onto his back. As soon as she did, Zeus made for the ocean with the young girl having no choice but to hold onto him. He swam to Crete with her on his back. Here, he had his way with her, and she became pregnant.

However, Zeus and Europa's relationship was no brief fling. She received special gifts from him, and the couple had three sons, all of whom grew up to become successful kings. One of them was Minos of Knossos, the magnificent palace on Crete. Europa also had the continent named after her, and she was one of the few lovers to escape Hera's wrath (Gleimius, 2022).

Io

When Zeus fell in love with the mortal Argive princess Io, he went down to Earth and put a big black cloud into the sky so that Hera wouldn't see him. However, the goddess noticed the obstruction and, somehow, knew her husband was involved. When she couldn't find him anywhere on Mount Olympus, she went down to the mortal realm and ordered the clouds to go.

The various versions of this story don't agree on what happened next. Some say that Zeus turned Io into a beautiful cow to prevent his wife from discovering them. Others state that the princess transformed herself to avoid Hera's wrath. A third version says that it was Hera who cursed Io to become a cow.

In the version of the story where Zeus is responsible for the transformation, Hera is not entirely convinced by the ruse, so she orders her husband to give her the cow as a gift. She then placed Argus, a giant who had 100 eyes, in charge of her prize to keep Io separated from Zeus. Because the monstrous guard had so many eyes, some were always awake and alert to watch Io and make sure she didn't escape.

Zeus then called in his son, Hermes, to kill Argus and free the cow. Hermes did this by lulling all 100 of the beast's eyes to sleep with his pipe of reeds. As for Io, Hera retaliated by sending a gadfly to taunt her—still in her animal form—continually until it drove her to wander from country to country, acting like a mad cow because of the incessant stinging. Zeus only returned Io to her human form when she reached Egypt. There, she eventually married Telegonus, the king of Egypt, with whom she had a family (Clementi, 2009; Greeka.com, 2024).

Alcmene

Alcmene, the daughter of Electryon, the king of Mycenae, was another mortal who was renowned for her beauty. Due to her virtuous, chaste nature, Zeus resorted to trickery to sleep with her, as he had with Europa. After watching her for some time, Zeus decided to act on his desires. He disguised himself as Alcmene's husband (or betrothed, according to some accounts), Amphitryon, who was away. The god convinced her by sharing details about her husband's wars and showing her souvenirs from his battles.

Soon afterward, Amphitryon returned. He found out what had happened but forgave his wife for her infidelity, as he realized that she had been tricked. Alcmene then gave birth to twins, one of whom was the son of

Zeus and the other of her husband. The former, as detailed in Chapter 2, grew up to become the famous demigod Heracles.

Callisto

Callisto was a naiad—a nymph of flowing freshwater sources. Like all the others of her kind, she was known for her beauty, charm, and caring nature. She was a follower of Artemis and had sworn an oath of chastity to the deity. She often visited Mount Olympus as part of the goddess's retinue, which was how Zeus met her. He eventually seduced her by shape-shifting into Artemis. The goddess discovered what had happened after she saw Callisto bathing and realized that she was pregnant. As a consequence, she expelled Zeus's unwitting lover from her group of virgin followers.

Alone and abandoned in the forest, Callisto gave birth to a son, Arcas. However, things then went from bad to worse for the nymph when, in revenge, Hera turned her into a brown bear. As he had done with Io, Zeus sent Hermes to take the baby to his mother, Maia (another of Zeus's lovers), to be raised in safety. Eventually, Callisto, still a bear, met her son when he nearly killed her. Zeus intervened again by reuniting mother and son in the sky as the constellations Ursa Major (Callisto) and Ursa Minor (Arcas).

Ganymede

While the majority of Zeus's lovers were women, in ancient Greece, there was a strong tradition of older men having sexual relations with adolescent boys. Zeus was also said to participate in this custom, with Ganymede being the most famous of his male lovers.

Homer describes the young man as being one of the most beautiful mortals and tells of how the gods abducted him and took him to Mount Olympus, where he served as Zeus's cupbearer. According to the ancient poet, he "was the loveliest born of the race of mortals, and therefore the gods caught him away to themselves, to be Zeus's wine-pourer, for the sake of his beauty, so he might be among the immortals" (Lattimore, 1951). The story of Zeus and Ganymede is also told in the "Homeric Hymn to Aphrodite."

According to legend, Ganymede was the son of Tros or Laomedon, the king of Troy. He is said to have either been carried off by the gods, as described above, or by Zeus, who was disguised as an eagle. According to a Cretan version of the story, King Minos delivered him to serve as Zeus's servant. By way of compensation, Zeus gave Ganymede's father either a stud of immortal horses or a golden vine.

The earliest versions of Ganymede's story did not have an erotic dimension, but, by the fifth century B.C.E., it was widely believed that Zeus was attracted to him, and the story became a popular topic on Attic vases produced in this century. Notably, Socrates also reports that Zeus was in love with Ganymede (White, 1993).

Aphrodite's Affairs: Romance, Passion, and Jealousy

Aphrodite was the goddess of love, so it seems entirely appropriate that she would have had many relationships, despite being married to the smith god Hephaestus. She intervened in the lives of mortals and also had numerous affairs with her fellow gods, including Dionysus and Hermes. With the latter, she conceived the fertility deities Hermaphroditus and Priapos. She also had affairs with Nerites, a young sea god, Poseidon, and Zeus.

One of her most well-known affairs was with Ares, who she had a long-lasting relationship. This even outlasted her marriage, and, during that time, she had four divine sons with the god of war: Eros (not to be confused with the god born shortly after Chaos), Anteros, Deimos, and Phobos, and a daughter, Harmonia.

Everyone on Mount Olympus knew about Aphrodite and Ares's relationship, apart from her husband. When Helios finally told him, Hephaestus was humiliated and used his skills as a smith to get his revenge. He fashioned a gold mesh, which he used to catch the couple while they were making love. He then displayed them for all to see. His actions made the two the laughingstock among the gods and helped heal Hephaestus's wounded pride (Monaghan, 1999).

Another of Aphrodite's most famous relationships was her affair with the handsome mortal Adonis, whom she was forced to share with Persephone, the wife of Hades and queen of the underworld. Their dispute over him was so contentious that they eventually turned to Zeus for judgment. He decided, with the help of Calliope, one of the Muses, that Adonis should spend four months of the year with each woman and have the remaining four to himself. Because he favored Aphrodite, Adonis spent those spare months with her. However, eventually, he was killed by a boar, and the goddess created the first red rose in her attempt to save her lover. See the full story below.

Eros and Psyche: A Fairy Tale in Ancient Greece

Eros was the son of Aphrodite and the Greek god of love and sex. The tale of his love affair with Psyche, a mortal princess, and the deification of the human soul, was at first a part of Greco-Roman folklore before eventually being committed to literature in Lucius Apuleius's second-century C.E. Latin novel, *The Golden Ass*. He is usually depicted as a fat-winged child, but in this account, Eros is represented as a young adult.

The story tells of Eros and Psyche's attempt to find love and trust with one another. Aphrodite was jealous of the young girl's beauty, as men were leaving their altars barren to worship a mortal woman instead of the goddess. In revenge, she encouraged her son to cause her rival to fall in love with the ugliest creature on Earth. However, Eros fell in love with Psyche instead and spirited her away to his home.

Their happiness was ruined by a visit from the girl's jealous sisters. They caused her to betray her husband's trust by planting doubt in her mind. Her actions wounded Eros emotionally and physically, and he left his wife. A devastated Psyche then wandered the globe, looking for her lost love. She visited the Temple of Demeter and the Temple of Hera to get advice. Eventually, she happened upon the Temple of Aphrodite and approached the goddess to ask her for help.

Aphrodite set Psyche four tasks, which she completed with supernatural assistance. The deity then relented and Zeus, after having a near-death experience, turned Psyche into an immortal so that she could live among the gods with her husband, Eros. They went on to have a daughter, Voluptas or Hedone (meaning "bliss" or "physical pleasure").

Star-Crossed Lovers: Tragic Romances of Greek Myth

Many Greek romances are tragic, which is unsurprising given that so many ancient writers such as Sophocles, Euripides, and Aeschylus are renowned for their tragic plays. Some of the examples we've just explored have tragic dimensions. For example, as described above, Artemis banished Callisto after she became pregnant by the king of the gods. Hera then transformed her into a bear, Hermes separated her from her son, and eventually, Zeus turned her into a star in the sky. Meanwhile, Io wandered the continents for several years as a cow.

Several more famous examples of tragic Greek romances are explored below.

Orpheus and Eurydice

The story of Orpheus and Eurydice is one of the most tragic love stories in Greek mythology. Orpheus of Thrace was part divine, as he was the son of Apollo and the Muse Calliope. He was famous for his musical talents with the lyre, a gift he inherited from his mother. He is also remembered for his love of Eurydice.

The couple lived happily together until one day, while Eurydice was wandering in the forest with nymphs, she encountered the shepherd Aristaeus, who made unwanted advances toward her. As she was fleeing from his amorous attention, a poisonous snake bit and killed her, leaving her husband heartbroken.

Destroyed by the loss, Orpheus turned to music. His mournful melodies moved the gods, and, consequently, they allowed him to travel to the underworld to find his departed wife. He was able to enter this realm by enchanting the guard dog Cerberus with his lyre, as you may recall from Chapter 2.

When he arrived at his destination, the musician played his sorrowful songs to the god of the dead and his wife, Persephone. As a result, Hades allowed Orpheus to return to the land of the living with Eurydice on condition that he lead her out of the underworld without turning to look at her. But as the couple were making their exit, he stopped hearing her footsteps behind him and became worried, thinking that the gods had fooled him. He lost his faith and turned to look back, which meant that Eurydice stayed behind.

Orpheus had to return to the mortal realm without her, but he was devastated and felt he could not live without his wife, so he called for his own death in song. His wish was granted. Some stories say that wild beasts or the maenads (the female followers of Dionysus) tore him apart. Another story has it that Zeus killed him with a lightning bolt.

Aphrodite and Adonis

Another tragic Greek love story is that of Aphrodite and Adonis. The mortal man's grandmother, Cenchreis, boasted that her daughter Myrrah was more beautiful than the goddess of love. Infuriated by the woman's arrogance, Aphrodite cursed the girl so that Myrrah fell in love with her father and Cenchreis's husband, King Theias.

The lovestruck girl would sneak into Theias's room at night, and the two would make love. As their liaisons always took place in the dark, the king was unaware that he was having an affair with his daughter. But one night, he lit a lamp and discovered the identity of the mystery woman. Horrified, he tried to kill her, but she escaped.

Soon after Myrrah fled, she discovered that she was pregnant. She did not wish to live, but she did not want to die either, so she begged the gods to end her suffering. She got her wish when she was transformed into a myrrh tree. One day, a boar found it and struck it with his tusks, creating a tear from which Adonis was born.

At the same moment that the infant sprung out of the tree, Aphrodite was walking past. She took the baby and gave it to Persephone to look after. He grew up to be the most handsome man among mortals and gods alike. Consequently, both the goddess of love and Adonis's foster mother fell in love with him.

Both women were determined to have him to themselves. They took their dispute to Zeus, who referred them to the Muse Calliope. She decided and Zeus decreed that Adonis should spend a third of the year with one and a third with the other. He could spend the remainder of the time as he wished. He favored Aphrodite, so he spent his free months with her. When he was with Persephone in the underworld, plants died, and winter took place on Earth.

Hunting would prove to be Adonis's undoing. One day, he came across a wild boar, which he struck with his spear. The beast then retaliated by impaling him with its tusks. Aphrodite rushed in to rescue him. In her attempt to save him, she pricked her toe with the thorn of a white rose. However, she was too late, and her lover died. It is said that the petals were stained with the blood of the goddess, creating the first red rose.

Summary

The love stories of Greek mythology do not offer an ideal view of romance by modern standards.

Notably, Zeus is often said to have tricked his wife to try and stop her from finding out about his infidelities, and in many tales, he deceived his lovers—many of whom were chaste, virtuous women—into sleeping with him. It's extraordinary that the immortal king of the gods had to resort to trickery to seduce so many women when, with his looks, strengths, and status, he should have been able to have anyone he wanted. These myths thus underscore his position of authority and power as a patriarch, and they reflect the ancient Greek view that women were in a subservient societal role and were seen as men's playthings, easily used and discarded.

Our exploration of these stories highlights their focus on true love, passion, and power. The examples discussed in this chapter also cast a light on the complexities of human relationships and the diversity of human experience in Greek myth, as well as how all these themes continue to resonate in contemporary society. The tragic romances, then, emphasize loss, longing, unrequited love, and the often-painful consequences of desire, illustrating the dual nature of this phenomenon as a source of profound joy and deep sorrow.

Beyond this, the Greek love stories reflect not only the dynamics between men and women but also gender fluidity, as gods and mortals alike change forms and cross the boundaries between the masculine and feminine. The tales we encounter also draw parallels to the contemporary challenge to rigid gender norms that has unfolded over the past few centuries.

Now that we have concluded this discussion on love and beauty, we will meet their opposite: Monsters.

Chapter 4

Mythical Creatures:

Meet the Beasts

Take courage, my heart:
you have been through worse than this. □
Be strong, saith my heart;
I am a soldier;
I have seen worse sights than this.

–Homer, from "The Odyssey"

Greek mythology is full of stories about the marriages and liaisons between many creatures. Some mythical unions produced hybrid beasts; in many cases, they were hideously ugly and greedy for human flesh. Often, the gods used these terrifying monsters to punish theire enemies or attack people who made them angry. Usually, it took a hero like Perseus or Heracles to kill them and strip them of their powers.

However, not all beasts were bad. Some, like the centaurs, were cultured, and the giant Cyclopes were the allies of Zeus. Triton, a merman and demigod, also looked out for others. Another example is the griffin, a mythical animal with a lion's body and an eagle's wings and head. This hybrid creature acted as a guardian to the gods, watching over Apollo's treasures and Dionysus's bowl of wine.

We explore some of the stories and their significance below.

The Famous Monsters of Greek Myth

Centaurs

These wild creatures had the heads and upper torsos of men but were horses from the waist down, and they had proficient skills in everything from music to medicine. Their characters were as mixed as their bodies. They were usually gentle and wise, and they provided wisdom to the heroes Jason and Perseus. On the other hand, they could also be warlike, fighting many famous battles. One example is their conflict with the Lapiths, a legendary people who, although human in form, were said to be brothers to the centaurs.

Satyrs

The satyrs were part man, part animal, and the children of nymphs and goats. As such, they were nature spirits of the woods and mountains. According to another account, they were originally human, but Hera transformed them into their hybrid shape out of anger that they were not guarding Dionysus properly. As companions of the latter god, they loved drinking and reveling, chasing nymphs, and scaring forest visitors.

Cyclopes

The Cyclopes were giants that each had a single eye in their foreheads. There are three distinct groups. Thanks to Hesiod, we know that the first three, Brontes, Steropes, and Arges, were the sons of Gaia and Uranus. In Homer's Odyssey, when Odysseus encounters them, they are depicted as uncivilized shepherds who are the brethren of Polyphemus, Poseidon's son and a one-eyed giant himself. Another story has them as the builders of the Cyclopean walls of Mycenae and Tiryns.

According to Hesiod's account, the first of the Cyclopes existed before many of the gods. After the Titans came into being, they took the giants' power and banished them to the underworld. Zeus eventually released them from their imprisonment there and, in return, they helped him during the Titanomachy. After Zeus had won the struggle and was installed on Mount Olympus, they became his royal blacksmiths. Notably, they made his thunderbolts and Poseidon's helmets.

Hydras

The Hydra of Lerna was a lake-dwelling serpentine monster. As you may recall from Chapter 2, one of the 12 impossible tasks that the hero Heracles completed was the defeat of this beast with assistance from his nephew. This was a nine-headed dragon that had acquired its additional eight heads over time, as when one was cut off, two more grew to replace it.

Automatons

We don't tend to associate the ancient Greeks with technological advancements, but did you know that engineered beasts feature in Greek mythology? Indeed, automatons (or automata) make several appearances in this mythical canon.

Interestingly, we get the Latin "automaton" from the ancient Greek word αὐτόματον, meaning "acting of one's own will." Homer first used the term in the Iliad to describe a door opening automatically and the mechanical movement of wheeled tripods.

Hephaestus created animate metallic statues for his workshop, some of which were men, animals, and monsters. There was also Talos, an artificial man Hephaestus built from bronze after Zeus commissioned him to do so. He was said to circle Crete three times a day to protect the island from invaders (Spicer, 2023). Meanwhile, King Alcinous of the Phaeacians is said to have employed gold and silver watchdogs.

Additionally, Aristotle tells of how Daedalus used quicksilver (mercury) to make his wooden statue of Aphrodite move. In On Aristotle on the Soul, Philoponus reports (van der Eijk, 2006: 35):

> He says "they say the same thing as the comic poet Philip, who said that Daedalus made a wooden Aphrodite that moved"; for after making some hollows in the statue Daedalus poured quicksilver in, so that the quicksilver by its motion (for it is very easily moved and continuously rolling

over and by its own pushing causes movement to the statue) made the statue of Aphrodite appear moving of its own accord.

Other Greek legends tell of the inventor using the same technique to install voices in his moving statues.

Minotaur

The Minotaur was born on Crete and was a part bull, part man that ate humans. King Minos ordered his craftsman, Daedalus, to build a labyrinth to imprison the creature. Going back to Chapter 2, you may remember that Theseus eventually put the beast to death with the help of Ariadne.

Monstrous Females

Greek myth also has its fair share of monstrous females. We explore some of these below.

Medusa

Medusa was one of the daughters of the sea god Phorcys and his sister Ceto. Three of their offspring were the Gorgons, the other two being Stheno and Euryale. These women were terrifying: They had snakes instead of hair and bodies covered in scales. Their gaze was so deadly that it could turn anyone who looked into their eyes to stone. In the words of Aeschylus (2008: 531) in Prometheus Bound "the Gorgons, winged / With snakes for hair—hatred of mortal man."

The most famous of the Gorgons was Medusa. She was the favorite of her father, who gave her the power to transform herself into a beautiful woman. In return, she sacrificed her immortality. According to one story, the sisters had serpents growing from their heads because Athena was so jealous of Medusa's beauty that she turned the strands of her rival's hair into snakes (Wilkinson, 1998).

The Gorgons lived in an underground cave guarded by their sisters, the Graeae. The names of the three summed up their characters. They were Pemphedro (Spiteful), Deino (Terrible), and Enyo (Warlike). They shared one tooth and one eye among them.

As we saw in Chapter 2, Perseus was confident that he could behead Medusa. However, he also knew it would not be easy. So, due to the difficulty of this task, he enlisted the help of the gods, receiving enchanted objects from Hermes, Hades, and Athena. So equipped, the hero flew to the Gorgon's home with Hermes's winged sandals and used the invisible helmet from the god of the underworld to trick the Graeae. He then used the shield so that he could avoid making eye contact with his target. Finally, he beheaded Medusa with his sword. In his quest, he was also assisted by the one eye the grey-haired sisters shared.

The story of the infamous Gorgon demonstrates how ancient and modern commentators demonize female rage and power. It also shows how a woman may be rendered monstrous to stop audiences from questioning the behavior of men. Early versions of Medusa's myth do not record this detail, but ancient objects of art show her as a beautiful maiden, not a horrid monster. These renderings predate the works of Hesiod, Aeschylus, and Ovid.

At some point, though, depictions of Medusa shifted from an attractive young woman to a hideous beast. They present her as both an aggressor and a victim by portraying her as a tragic figure in death. The earliest such rendition appears on vase art created by Polygnotus, who drew her as a beautiful woman peacefully sleeping as Perseus beheads her. The act of killing a slumbering maiden is not heroic. It has therefore been proposed that these vases were either intended to elicit sympathy for her fate or to mock the hero (Karoglou, 2018).

The Sirens

The Sirens were another hybrid creature, as they had the bodies of birds and the heads of women. They were renowned for their song, which was said to be so seductive that it distracted sailors and caused shipwrecks (Wilkinson, 1998).

In the Odyssey, a group of these women attacked Odysseus and his men on their travels. To make sure that his ship wasn't destroyed, he ordered his men to stuff their ears with wax so that they wouldn't be enthralled. However, he still wanted to hear, so he tied himself to the mast as his crew sailed safely by.

The Harpies

These were birds with women's heads and sharp talons who lived on islands in the Aegean, where they preyed on people's souls. In myth, the Thracian king, Phineus, displeased the gods, so they sent the Harpies to pick at his eyes and steal his food. He was saved when Jason and the

Argonauts (see Chapter 2) came to Thrace and had the North Wind's son chase away the creatures.

The Sphinx

The Sphinx was the daughter of Echidna, a snake-like monster known as the mother of all monsters who lived with the giant Typhon. Their other children were the Chimera, the Hydra, and Cerberus. In Greek myth, the Sphinx is merciless and treacherous. She has the head of a woman, the haunches of a lion, and the wings of a bird. In both Greek and Egyptian myths, she is often depicted as a guardian of temples and other similar sites.

In the Greek myth and drama of Oedipus, the Sphinx is sent to punish the people of Thebes, who had displeased the gods. The monster ate anyone who could not answer the riddle: "Which animal has at first four legs, then two legs, then three legs?" (Wilkinson, 1998: 67).

No one could come up with the answer until Oedipus realized that it was a human who crawls as a baby, walks on two legs as an adult, and moves around with a stick in old age. When the Sphinx heard the answer, she threw herself to her death on some jagged rocks.

Deeper Meanings: When Concepts Become Creatures

The purpose of mythology across time and place is to make sense of the world and provide insight into why things are the way they are, including everything from natural phenomena like the weather and volcanic eruptions to human behavior and society. So, Greek mythology also describes battles with monsters alongside stories of the lives of gods and heroes and their love affairs. The monsters we encountered above are entirely fictional, but they were created to explain conflicts and difficult times, thereby serving to bring order to a chaotic and uncertain world.

Monsters appear frequently in this canon. Examples, many of which we've discussed, include the Minotaur, the Chimera, the Gorgons, the Hydra, the Sphinx, and the Sirens and Harpies. There were also giants, centaurs, satyrs, werewolves, man-made beasts, and vampiric phantoms. What all of these diverse beings have in common is that they pose a threat to society and must be defeated. They require gods and heroes to protect humans against them and maintain the status quo.

While fearsome creatures often walked among the people, they tended to be found on the outskirts of the known world. For example, the Minotaur was imprisoned underground in a maze while many sea monsters are found in the oceans bordering distant lands. Monsters, in this sense, act as fantasies or warnings about the sort of people likely to be encountered on a journey into the unknown—as exemplified by Odysseus on his voyage home or by the adventures of Jason and the Argonauts. They also serve as a way to explore the limits of human behavior, as is the case with those monsters that eat human beings, like the sea serpents Scylla and Charybdis (Rae, 2010).

Why Are So Many Monsters Female?

It is also significant that so many Greek monsters are female. Classicist Debbie Felton (2013) proposes that these creatures "spoke to men's fear of women's destructive potential. The myths then, to a certain extent, fulfill a male fantasy of conquering and controlling the female." This observation helps explain why depictions of Medusa shifted from a beautiful young woman to a villainous Gorgon over time.

Tales about monstrous women may be representative of ancient male authors' regard for the opposite sex. For example, in his first-century epic *Metamorphoses*, the Roman poet Ovid wrote about Medusa and her fearsome nature while in Homer's *Odyssey*, composed in the seventh or eighth century B.C.E., the Greek hero Odysseus is tasked with choosing between fighting Scylla and Charybdis, both beautiful women transformed into terrifying sea creatures (McGreevy, 2021). The fact that these monsters are female is significant and suggestive of men's hidden fears and desires surrounding women.

In *Women and Other Monsters: Building a New Mythology* (2021), Jess Zimmerman argues that the qualities that made these female creatures "monstrous" to the ancient Greeks were their greatest strengths. Notably, the traits that they represent, such as aspiration, knowledge, strength, and desire, are not hideous and have always been viewed as heroic when expressed in men. Thus, the gender of so many Greek monsters may simply represent the fear surrounding powerful women.

Summary

Like gods, the many monsters in Greek mythology can be good or bad or have benign or malicious intentions. It is also apparent that many are female, perhaps reflecting how men perceived empowered women.

They often also take the role of a guardian or gatekeeper, testing the worthiness of questing characters before allowing them to progress to the next stage of their quests. They demand that heroes demonstrate the ability to confront and conquer fearsome adversaries. Apart from adding obvious dramatic tension to a tale, creatures like the Hydra, the Minotaur, and Medusa also embody human fears and societal anxieties. Their narratives often convey deeper moral and philosophical lessons, such as the importance of bravery, quick thinking, and perseverance.

Moving on from these mythical creatures that serve as symbols of chaos and the unknown, the next chapter explores another fascinating part of Greek mythology, namely, its myths surrounding the creation of the universe.

Chapter 5

The Creation Myths:

Origins of the Universe

Of all creatures that can feel and think,
we women are the worst treated things alive.

– Euripides

Pandora would certainly have agreed with this observation from Euripides. According to one ancient Greek creation myth, she was the first woman and also the being responsible for bringing many evils to humankind. In that sense, her role in human creation has significant parallels with Eve's.

In addition to Pandora's tale, the ancient Greeks told many other stories about the origins of the universe and mankind. In this chapter, we retell some of these and analyze them to better understand why this civilization told the stories they did.

The Creation Myth

Our knowledge of the ancient Greek origin story comes from some of the land's earliest literary sources, namely Hesiod's *Theogony* and *Works and Days*.

The ancient poet tells us that at the beginning, there was Chaos, the personification of absolute nothingness, an immense, dark void that the world emerged from. This contained the seeds of everything, including the earth, the seas, the heavens, and the gods, but nothing existed yet. Then, suddenly, came Gaia—Mother Earth. From her came Uranus, the god of the sky, and many other primordial gods, including Ourea, the god of the mountains, and Pontus, the god of the sea.

Also from Chaos came Eros, the god of procreation and love, whose early birth is a demonstration of how the ancient Greeks considered love to be one of the most vital powers in the world. In later tradition, this primordial being was made the son of Aphrodite, who we encountered in Chapter 3. However, both origin stories for Eros existed in the Greek world.

After this, Tartarus was born. He was a dark place, like the personification of an abyss, and was the first god of the underworld. Next came Erebus, the god of darkness, and Nyx, the goddess of the night. All were born from the original nothingness.

The Titans

Although the universe had now been created, there was no one to enjoy it. So, Gaia took her son Uranus as her husband and produced a race of

12 supernatural beings called the Titans. They were the first generation of gods to follow their primordial parents and were the predecessors to the Olympian gods. As you may recall from Chapter 1, the six male Titans were Cronus, Oceanus, Coeus, Hyperion, Iapetus, and Crius, while the six Titanesses were Rhea, Tethys, Theia, Phoebe, Themis, and Mnemosyne.

Gaia and Uranus produced six more children, but these were very different from the Titans. First came the three Cyclopes (see Chapter 4). Then Mother Earth gave birth to the three Hecatoncheires, each with 50 heads and 100 arms. Each of his powerful, terrifying offspring frightened their father, so Uranus imprisoned the Titans, the Cyclopes, and the Hecatoncheires in the deepest depths of the earth—Gaia's body—and bound them tightly with chains so that they could not escape.

Gaia was horrified by the way her husband had treated their children, so she took her revenge. She made a deadly weapon, a stone sickle, and visited the Titans in their underground prison. She told them her plan and asked them to help her. Each of them hesitated, but eventually, the youngest Titan, Cronus, agreed to help her and defeat his father.

She freed Cronus and hid him near her. When darkness fell and Uranus returned to Gaia, their son burst from his hiding place and castrated his father with the stone sickle. Uranus's horrible wounds spurted three dark drops of blood that fell to Earth and turned into terrible beings called the Three Furies. These female spirits roamed the planet and took revenge on those who had offended the gods by driving them insane for their crimes. Another drop of the god of the sky's blood landed in the sea, where it turned into thick white foam. From that emerged the goddess of love, Aphrodite.

The Olympians

Ultimately, Cronus coupled with Rhea, and they produced the 12 Olympian gods who the ancient Greeks worshipped. Like his father before him, Cronus felt threatened by his offspring. So, he ate each one whole after they were born, apart from Zeus, who Rhea had managed to hide from her husband. The story has it that, following a 10-year power struggle known as the Titanomachy, Zeus, together with his siblings defeated the Titans and claimed their rightful role as rulers of the world.

After their victory, the Olympian gods divided up the cosmos. Poseidon ruled the sea, Hades the underworld, and Zeus the heavens.

The Creation of Humankind

The Greeks told many different stories about the creation of humankind. In one account, humanity came about when an ancestor called Pelasgus appeared out of the soil Another story tells of how Zeus created a series of different races to occupy Earth. First came the good men of the Golden Age, followed by the violent Silver Race. Afterward, came the metalworkers of the Age of Bronze, the Race of Heroes, and, finally, our Age of Iron.

Two of the most well-known ancient Greek creation myths are the intertwined stories of Prometheus and Pandora, which we explore below.

The Theft of Fire and the Punishment of Prometheus

Prometheus, whose name means "the foreseeing," was a Titan and the son of Iapetus and his wife, one of the daughters of Oceanus—a son of Uranus and Gaia and father to the river gods and the Oceanids. Prometheus occupies a unique position in Greek mythology as the first champion of man and the creator of the human race. He is also known as a fire god and a divine trickster.

Creating the First Men

Prometheus is said to have shaped the first men out of clay at Panopea in Boeotia, a region of modern-day Greece. He then persuaded Athena, whose birth he had assisted, to breathe life into the clay images (Stapleton, 1986).

The Theft of Fire

Another version of the story says that man already existed and that Prometheus acted as the champion of mankind, promoting their interests to the gods.

One example of this is how he used trickery to ensure that man would have the better part of any sacrifice made to the gods. He did this by making two bundles of meat out of the carcass of an ox. He wrapped the fat around the hide and bone of one bundle while he used the stomach to make the other, putting the best meat inside. He then asked Zeus to make a choice between the two. Naturally, the king of the gods picked the succulent-looking bundle made up of the scraps. By doing so, he left man with the better part of the sacrificial meat (Stapleton, 1986).

Angered by the ruse, Zeus hid the knowledge of how to make fire from mankind so that they could not cook the meat, rendering their prize useless. Prometheus then stuck up for humans again. He stole fire from Mount Olympus—Aeschylus specifies that he took it from the forge of Hephaestus. After bringing this to Earth, Prometheus began to teach mortals everything that made them better than other animals. The skills he taught them included how to build, how to use metals and tools, how to understand the position of the stars, and how to use herbs for healing.

As he watched all this from Mount Olympus, Zeus became very angry. He decided to punish Prometheus by creating the first woman. This was Pandora, who was made to destroy mankind. This story is told below.

The Punishment of Prometheus

As we will see, Zeus's plot to destroy mankind failed, but he did not lose his desire to punish Prometheus for his insubordination and keenness to champion the interests of humans. Although the almighty Olympian could no longer bring about their end, he could still punish the supreme trickster and make him submit to his will.

In addition to retribution for the crimes outlined above, Zeus also wanted to torture Prometheus because he knew a secret that could be detrimental to the stability of the world. This was that Thetis, one of the Nereids, would give birth to a son who was destined to be greater than his father. As both Zeus and his brother Poseidon fancied the nymph, there was a real chance that she could bear a divine son that would threaten the peace and end Zeus's reign as king of the gods (Stapleton, 1986). It is unclear whether Prometheus learned about this from Thetis or if he instinctively knew this information as the one who foresaw all.

Zeus was aware of part of the prophecy and that Prometheus was keeping something from him, but he could not act unless he could get the truth out of him. So, he had Prometheus seized by Kratos (strength) and Bia (force) and had him taken to the mountains of the Caucasus. On Zeus's orders, Hephaestus chained the prisoner to a high rock. Bound, Prometheus was exposed to the mountain cold at night and was tormented by day by a vulture his imprisoner had sent, which tore into his liver. His wound healed at night, and the cycle continued day in and day out. Prometheus was doomed to perpetual agony unless he revealed his secret, but he bravely refused.

The original myth tells us that Prometheus was to remain chained to the rock for eternity. However, this went against the Greek sense of justice that the champion of mankind should suffer forever, so a solution was eventually found.

The newer version of the myth says that, ultimately, Heracles eventually freed Prometheus and that the centaur Chiron gave him his immortality. This was the result of an exchange. The centaur was in increasing pain from a wound he had unintentionally received from the hero, so he accepted Prometheus's mortality so that he could die in peace. Prometheus was then reconciled with Zeus and told him the secret upon which the maintenance of order depended.

Pandora's Box: The Origin of Human Suffering

Pandora, whose name means "all-giving" was the first woman and was created as a punishment for the theft of fire. Having witnessed Prometheus's action on Earth, Zeus sent for Hephaestus and ordered him to make a woman out of clay. He then commanded Athena to breathe life into her, and he called on the rest of the gods to make her beautiful and irresistible to men.

Zeus then sent Pandora to the mortal realm with a sealed jar (or box). He planned that she would destroy mankind, but he knew Prometheus would know better than to accept a gift from the gods. The Olympian realized that Prometheus's brother, Epimetheus, a name meaning "afterthought," would be more easily fooled. As anticipated, he accepted Pandora and married her despite his brother's warnings (Stapleton, 1986; Wilkinson, 1998).

Then, as Prometheus had feared, Pandora opened the jar and disaster came upon man. Eventually, she wanted to see what was inside, so she lifted the lid. All the ills and fears of humanity escaped, with only hope left inside when she closed it again. Because this virtue remained, man still had the will to go on despite all the bad things in the world, as this deceives him that all will be okay. Thus, because of a woman's curiosity, Zeus's plan had almost succeeded, but her action ultimately foiled it.

Another, later version of the story says that the jar contained blessings instead of evil and that the contents escaped and returned to Mount Olympus (Wilkinson, 1998). Similarly to the preceding account, these blessings would have been preserved for the human race had they not been lost because of Pandora's interest in what the jar contained.

Analyzing the Prometheus and Pandora Myths

The main source of the Prometheus and Pandora myths is Hesiod. He tells the story twice, once in *Theogony* and again in *Works and Days.* The two versions differ from one another, both in details and emphasis, but they are variants of the same tale.

Hesiod uses the myth in *Theogony* to explain the creation of women and the reason for their duplicitous nature. He describes Pandora in the following terms (1987: 591–594): "For from her is the race of women and female kind: of her is the deadly race and tribe of women who live amongst mortal men to their great trouble, no helpmeets in hateful poverty, but only in wealth."

Hesiod characterizes her as a *kalon kakon* meaning "the beautiful-evil thing," painting her as beautiful, good, and noble but lacking in virtue. This means that, aesthetically, Pandora has a beautiful ugliness and, morally, a noble evil.

Additionally, as a creation of the gods, Pandora's beauty makes her a dangerous object. On the one hand, she is a marvel, on the other, she is the manifestation of falsehood, as her appearance hides a hidden evil. Her wickedness is due to her falseness, as she is deceptive by nature due to the purpose Zeus had in mind when he engineered her creation. Also, her beauty was deliberately designed to hide the corruption she contains.

Pandora causes wonder due to her beauty, but this is also associated with the danger she represents. So, Hesiod implies that her external beauty hides something worse than emptiness, as it conceals an ongoing desire within her to consume and encourage the desire of her "victims." She appears to bear wealth to men due to her appearance and finery but, in reality, she is a vacuum (Boulding, 2015).

In *Works and Days*, the Prometheus and Pandora story is Hesiod's vision of the origin of evil and his explanation for the challenges of human existence, which is all too often plagued by labor and disease. In this text, he says that she was a "gigantic evil" created to unleash all hardships onto humanity. Before she existed, the world did not know poverty, disease, or sin (Morford & Lenardon, 2003).

She was created by the will of Zeus, who was determined to make a perfect maiden who would be irresistible to men and who would take the blame for the world's new evils. In other words, although the gods brought her to life to complete a task Zeus had set, Pandora alone receives the blame for the suffering inflicted on the world as willed by a god whose role in the situation is generally ignored.

However, scholars have not paid much attention to the figure of Pandora, preferring instead to celebrate Prometheus as the symbol of the heroic human spirit who dared to assert himself in defiance of the status quo his fellow gods had established. If they have to acknowledge the Pandora part of the myth, scholars simply see it as a platform for Hesiod's misogyny. But as the myth had a long tradition before the ancient poet recorded it, we cannot attribute this element to him alone.

Interestingly, before Hesiod told the patriarchal version of the Pandora story where a woman is responsible for the troubles of Earth and its people, she was known as a beneficent Earth goddess in oral tradition (Brown, 2014). However, other sources suggest that the deity of that name is unrelated to the woman who unintentionally unleashed evil on the world (Cartwright, 2015).

More recently, in *Women Who Run With Wolves* (1989), Clarissa Pinkola Estes argues that such tales and myths have often been interpreted questionably by influential psychologists (Estes, 1992: 47-48):

> Women's curiosity was given a negative connotation, whereas men were called investigative. Women were called nosy, whereas men were called inquiring. In reality, the trivialization of women's curiosity so that it seems like nothing more than irksome snooping denies women's insight, hunches, and intuitions. It denies all her senses. It attempts to attack her fundamental power.

In the myth of Pandora, the female protagonist serves a similar function. Thus, her story could be used to warn women against expressing curiosity and therefore keep them subservient to men.

Summary

Greek creation myths explained how the gods they worshipped came to power and to reside on Mount Olympus. They also explored why humankind was created and forced to endure all kinds of hardship and misfortune. These myths also exemplify the themes of order emerging from chaos, the cyclical nature of life, and the interplay between divine and mortal realms.

Notably, though, Greek myth tends to blame Pandora for bringing evil into the world, even though she did so due to the wishes of a man (Zeus). This had a long-lasting impact on the cultural taboos surrounding female curiosity, as women's pursuit of knowledge came to hold a negative connotation. It also had a heavy influence on later religions' demand that women be submissive and obedient followers of their husbands. There have been several feminist retellings of the Pandora myth, such as those by Barbara Walker and Adrienne Rich. Thus, understanding Greek mythology can help shed light on the origins of contemporary perceptions of gender.

In the next chapter, we look at the opposite of beginnings: the end.

Chapter 6

Death and the Afterlife:

Journeys to the Underworld

For Hades is mighty in calling men to account below the earth, and with a mind that records in tablets he surveys all things.

– Aeschylus

In this chapter, we explore ancient Greek beliefs, myths, and legends about death and the afterlife.

The ancient Greeks believed that when people died, their souls went to the underworld, the dark realm, also called Hades, after its ruler, who shared his domain with his queen, Persephone. In the world of the departed, the occupants were tried by three judges: Rhadamanthus, Minos, and Aeacus. If they found that the deceased had lived an evil life, that person might be punished.

The underworld had a unique geography and location. The early Greeks placed it beyond the River Oceanus, which encircled the world. Later on, it was thought that it was beneath the earth, hence the name. From myth, we know that it had rocks, caves, five rivers, two special areas—Erebos and

Tartarus—where souls were punished, and the Elysian Fields, the home of the blameless dead.

Below, we also look at the stories of heroes who traveled to the underworld and returned to Earth to tell the tale, as well as the themes of rebirth and regeneration in Greek myth.

The Underworld Deities

Hades

Hades was the god of the dead and the son of the Titans Cronus and Rhea. Although he was brother to Poseidon and Zeus and one of the 12 Olympians (see Chapter 1), he did not live on Mount Olympus but in the underworld, where he ruled over the dead. He was also the god of wealth and had rich mines under the earth. He was connected to the bounty of the fields through his marriage to Persephone, daughter of the harvest goddess Demeter.

Persephone

The goddess of spring and the queen of the underworld. During a visit to Earth, Hades caught sight of the fertility goddess Persephone, fell in love, carried her off in his chariot, and married her. Through this union, she became the co-ruler of the dark realm. However, her mother, Demeter, was angry and threatened to stop growing crops if her daughter was not returned to her. Eventually, Zeus intervened and agreed that Persephone should spend two-thirds of the year on Earth and the remainder with her husband.

Thanatos, Hypnos, and Morpheus: Death, Sleep, and Dreams

Hypnos was the Greek god of sleep. He was the son of Nyx (the primordial goddess of the night) and the twin of Thanatos (the personification of death). Among his many sons was Morpheus, who brought him the dreams of men. Meanwhile, Thanatos was the god or personified spirit of nonviolent death. The touch of the brothers was gentle; meanwhile, violent death was the domain of their sisters, the Keres, the spirits of disease and slaughter.

According to one version of Greek myth, Hypnos lived in the underworld, as did Thanatos. However, other versions say he lived elsewhere. Homer tells us that he lived on the island of Lemnos while Ovid says that he lived in a dark, musty cave in the land of the Cimmerians, through which flowed the water of the Lethe, the river of forgetfulness and oblivion (Britannica, 2024g).

Hecate

Hecate was the goddess of magic and ghosts. She was also the patron of magicians and witches. Although she lived in Hades, where she presided over spells and ceremonies, Hecate would come to Earth with her hounds and appear in various forms, including a she-wolf, a mare, or a woman with three bodies or heads. Often, she was seen at crossroads, where statues were erected to her.

Guardians of the Underworld

Another category of deities or supernatural creatures found in Hades were the guardians of the underworld: Charon, Cerberus, and the Furies.

Charon

To reach the underworld, the dead had to cross the river Acheron of Styx. They did this with the help of Charon, who ferried them across. He was a bad-tempered old man who insisted that everyone who traveled with him had to pay him one obol—a form of ancient currency. This is why the Greeks always put a coin in the mouths of the dead (Wilkinson, 1998).

Cerberus

Cerberus was Hades's three-headed dog and a guardian of the underworld. His parents were the monster Echidna, who was half-woman, half-snake, and Typhon, a fire-breathing giant whose body was covered with serpents and dragons. He also had numerous monstrous siblings, including Orthus, the Hydra of Lerna, and the Chimera (See Chapter 4 for more details).

Cerberus was kept at the gate of the underworld to prevent the living from getting in and frightening the souls of the dead as they entered. Not all ancient commentators agreed as to what he looked like. Apollodorus says that he was a strange mix of creatures, as he had three heads that resembled those of wild dogs, a dragon or serpent for a tail, and heads of snakes all over his back (Perseus Project, 2024). On the other hand, Hesiod (1987: 310) says that the beast had 50 heads and ate raw flesh: "A monster not to be overcome and that may not be described, Cerberus who eats raw flesh, the brazen-voiced hound of Hades, fifty-headed, relentless, and strong."

Regardless, by all accounts, the beast was a terrifying and off-putting watchdog and would certainly have scared off many mortals.

The Furies

The Three Furies or the Erinyes or Raging Ones lived deep in the underworld and tortured the souls of wrongdoers. Their names reflected their dark purpose. They were Tisiphone (Punishment), Megaera (Jealous Rage), and Allecto (Endless). As described in Chapter 5, they were born from the drops of blood that fell on Gaia when Cronos castrated Uranus. They were hideous to look at, and they had the bodies of old women, the heads of dogs, snakes for hair, jet-black skin, and bat wings on their backs.

The Kingdom of Hades: Denizens of the Underworld

The underworld had a unique geography entirely independent of Earth or Mount Olympus. We explore this mythical realm below.

The Rivers

The underworld had five rivers, all of which contributed to the terrible nature of the realm.

- **River Acheron:** This river of distress was full of stagnant, bitter water.

- **River Phlegethon:** This river contained liquid flames.

- **River Cocytus:** The wailing waters were haunted by the unburied dead who stayed there for 100 years.

- **River Styx:** The name of the longest river in the underworld translates to "hateful," and it circled the realm nine times.

- **River Lethe:** The dead drank from the waters of this river to forget their past lives.

The Three Realms of the Underworld

There were three main divisions in the underworld, with souls going to a certain area based on how they had behaved in life. The three main areas were Elysium, the Asphodel Meadows, and Tartarus.

Elysium

The earliest Greeks believed good people went to Elysium, also known as the Elysian Fields, which was ruled by the Titan Cronus after his death. The fields lay on the far side of the River Oceanus, which people thought encircled planet Earth. This was a beautiful place where dead souls were able to enjoy sports, poetry, and music.

Asphodel Meadows

The Asphodel Meadows is known as such because the adjective *asphodelòs* means "flowery," "fragrant," or "fertile" (Reece, 2009). This was where ordinary souls lived after death. In the *Odyssey*, Homer says that the Fields of Asphodel were close to the Land of Dreams and mentions that this is where the spirits of men who had abandoned their earthly labors dwelled. Thus, this was where people who had led mediocre lives resided in the afterlife. However, later writers saw it as a positive rather than a dull realm due to the positive associations between the Meadows and the asphodel flower. It also became the location of a few heroes, which changed its character to somewhere that was untouched, lovely, soft, and holy.

Tartarus

Tartarus, the third realm of the underworld, was where mortals were punished if they were judged to have misbehaved in life. It was an abyss located deep down, far below even the underworld. It was used as a dungeon to torment the wicked and served as a prison for the Titans, as you may recall from Chapter 5. In *Gorgias* (ca. 400 B.C.E.), Plato says that the wicked received divine punishment there.

Mortal Journeys to the Underworld

Usually, mortals did not travel to the underworld unless they had died. If they tried to visit the land of the departed while still alive, it was likely that they would never return to Earth. However, some did manage to make the journey and live to tell the tale. Their stories, which may be familiar from earlier chapters, are recounted below.

Orpheus

Orpheus famously traveled to the underworld so that he could reunite with his dead love, Eurydice, in the hope that she could return to Earth with him. While he successfully reached the dark realm and convinced its rulers to release his wife, Hades and Persephone told him that if he turned around to look at her on the way back, she would not be allowed to leave. However, he was unable to resist getting a glimpse of her, so she remained where she was.

See Chapters 2 and 3 for more about the tragic couple.

Heracles

Heracles visited the underworld to complete his last labor. See Chapter 2 for more details about all 12 of the hero's impossible tasks. His final deed was to capture Cerberus, the three-headed guardian of the realm, and take the beast to the Tiryns.

Before he traveled to the underworld, Heracles decided to take some extra precautions, as he knew that no mortal had ever returned from the land of the dead. He was also aware that once he entered the kingdom of Hades, he might not be allowed to leave and rejoin the living. So, he went to the city of Eleusis and saw Eumolpus, a priest and founder of the Eleusinian Mysteries. These were sacred religious rites that celebrated the myth of Demeter and her daughter, Persephone. It was believed that those who learned the secrets of those rituals would be happy in the underworld. After Heracles had met the conditions for membership, he was initiated into the cult (Perseus Project, 2024).

Then, Heracles came to a place called Taenarum in Laconia. There, he traveled through a deep, rocky cave to the underworld. Along the way, he encountered fellow heroes, monsters, and ghosts. He even competed in a wrestling contest. Finally, he found Hades and asked if he could take Cerberus. The god agreed to this on the condition that Heracles first overpower the beast with nothing more than brute strength.

The hero thus relinquished his weapons and went in search of Cerberus, finding him near the gates of the Acheron. After receiving a bite from the hound, Heracles was able to capture him by using his superhuman might to wrestle him to the ground. After he had completed his task of taking Cerberus to Eurystheus, who had set the labor, he returned the guardian of the underworld, unharmed, to his post at the entrance of the realm.

Odysseus

In Book 10 of the *Odyssey*, Odysseus and his men reach the island of Aeaea where Circe, a sorceress and the daughter of the sun god Helios and the Oceanid nymph Perse, advises him to travel to the underworld to consult with the spirit of the blind prophet Tiresias before continuing with his voyage.

Odysseus follows Circe's guidance in Book 11. In the underworld, he finds the prophet, who tells him that it is Poseidon who is preventing him from returning home. Tiresias warns the hero that, if his crew violate the cattle of the sun god Helios, the men will be lost, the difficulties of Odysseus's voyage will increase significantly, and upon his arrival home, he will find his house full of suitors, "insolent men" whom he will have to "atone in blood." He closes his prophecy by promising Odysseus a "rich old age" and "a seaborne death soft as this hand of mist" (Gifford & Seidman, 2008: 104).

As described by Homer, while in the underworld, Odysseus encounters many other spirits, including his mother and the heroes Agamemnon, Achilles, and Ajax. He also encounters Heracles, who is a phantom, not a spirit, as he rests among the immortal gods. This version of the hero tells Odysseus of his 12th labor, recounted above. Odysseus then returns to his ship and Circe's island.

Orpheus, Heracles, and Odysseus each had very different motivations for traveling to the underworld. Orpheus wanted to be reunited with his wife and bring her back to Earth, Heracles had to complete his 12th labor, and Odysseus sought advice from a prophet during a long and uncertain voyage. What they do have in common is that all three were mortal men who entered the realm alive and returned to Earth in the same condition.

Cycles of Rebirth and Regeneration in Greek Myth

Dying did not always mean staying in one part of the underworld forever. The ancient Greeks also believed in rebirth and regeneration of the spirit in select circumstances.

Those who entered the Elysian Fields had the choice of staying there or being born again. If a soul was reborn three times and gained access to the

Fields each time, he or she could enter the Isles of the Blessed and eternal paradise (Goddard, 2022).

The stories of Orpheus and Prometheus also explore the themes of rebirth and regeneration. In the story of Orpheus and Eurydice, he travels to the underworld to try and reclaim his dead wife and return to Earth with her. However, his attempt to bring her back to life ultimately failed (See Chapters 2 and 3).

The story of Prometheus's punishment also involves regeneration. When he was enduring Zeus's punishment by being exposed on a mountain in the Caucasus, he was also being tortured by a vulture that tore into his liver by day with the organ regenerating every night. This continued until Heracles released Prometheus and he received the gift of immortality from the centaur Chiron. See Chapter 5 for more details.

The Birth of Dionysus

Dionysus's name means "twice-born" because, according to Greek myth, he was quite literally birthed two times.

There are two different stories of Dionysus's birth. He was the son of Zeus and a mortal woman, Semele. The first legend says that as an infant, he was torn apart and eaten by the Titans. They consumed everything except his heart, as the organ was too tough and chewy. So, Semele drank a potion made from the remaining part of her son. The magic it was infused with impregnated her again, and after the organ pieces regenerated, he was reborn.

The second story says that a pregnant Semele pestered Zeus to acknowledge that he was the father of her unborn child. This angered the Olympian, who killed her with a lightning bolt. He then saved her unborn child, sewing it to his thigh to ensure that Dionysus could live.

Summary

The ancient Greeks believed that the underworld existed beneath the earth and had a complex geography. They also knew which deities and monsters resided there and about the different realms people might go to after their last judgment. These myths contribute to ongoing philosophical and ethical discussions about the nature of the soul, justice in the afterlife, and the moral implications of our actions in their exploration of existential questions around death and transition.

Other stories tell of the heroes who traveled to the land of the dead and managed to return to Earth afterward. Ancient Greek tradition also believed that rebirth and regeneration were possible in certain circumstances. Expanding on this theme, Chapter 7 explores metamorphosis, transformation, and shape-shifting in Greek myth.

Chapter 7
Metamorphosis Myths:
Transformations and Shape-Shifting

According to Greek mythology, humans were originally created with four arms, four legs, and a head with two faces. Fearing their power, Zeus split them into two separate parts, condemning them to spend their lives in search of their other halves.

— Plato

Transformation and shape-shifting are frequent occurrences in Greek myth, similar to their prevalence in mythologies, folklore, and visual arts originating from other ancient cultures. Stories of transformation are often linked to a time when the gods were the spirits of the land and natural phenomena.

Homer recorded some of the first instances of shape-shifting or metamorphosis in Greek myth in his epic, the *Iliad*. These examples involve a wide variety of transformations including those from human to animal and vice versa, from human to a plant or constellation, from inanimate object to person, and from one sex to another.

Antonis Chaliakopoulos (2021) observes that the transformations of gods often play an important role in the cults of various deities. Attempts to experience, commemorate, or re-enact the transformations that took place in Greek myth often played a key role in mystical rituals and folk celebrations.

In many tales, people are physically transformed through sorcery, spells, or divine intervention. Notably, many myths involve mortals being changed as a punishment for transgressions against the gods or as a reward for good deeds. We look at some of these stories below.

Godly Transformations

In some Greek myths, gods take on different forms to either deceive or test mortals. For example, Zeus commonly transformed himself to seduce mortal women and keep his amorous adventures secret from Hera—as described in Chapter 3. The gods also sometimes transformed themselves to achieve their goals. Zeus provides an excellent example again, as he transformed himself into an eagle to abduct the beautiful youth Ganymede from Troy so that he could serve as cupbearer on Mount Olympus.

Priapus

The story of the god Priapus demonstrates how transformation might be used to punish. He was a fertility god and the son of Aphrodite by Hermes, Dionysus, or Zeus.

At the same time that Paris, the Trojan prince, chose Aphrodite as the most beautiful of the goddesses, she was pregnant with Priapus. Jealous that the prince did not choose her, Hera used magic to deform the baby in her rival's womb, making him ugly and ill-tempered. In addition to his appearance, he was so hampered by his lust that he could hardly move. His obscene appearance and bad temperament alienated the other gods, who threw him down to Earth. Here, he became the companion of Pan, the god of the wild.

Gods Transforming Mortals—Causes and Consequences

Punishment

In Greek mythology, human transformation is usually a form of punishment from a god. For example, Zeus transformed King Lycaon and his children into wolves after the man killed and cooked his son, Nyctimus. Another example is Demeter, who transformed Ascalabus into a lizard for mocking her sadness and thirst in her search for her daughter Persephone.

King Midas

A more comic story involves King Midas, famous for wishing that everything he touched would turn to gold. In this instance, Apollo had won a contest with a flute player, Marsyas, to see who could play the most beautiful music. Midas said the god's victory was unfair, so Apollo punished him by giving him a pair of ass ears to embarrass him.

The king kept them hidden under his headdress. Only his barber knew his secret, but eventually, the man could keep it quiet no longer and, with no other humans around, told the earth. The nearby reeds heard and rustled the words: "Midas has ass's ears" (Wilkinson, 1998: 69).

In other stories, gods transform humans into animals because they are jealous of them or because they want to be their lovers.

Jealousy

The goddesses frequently transformed women that they were jealous of. For example, one of Artemis's mortal followers, Titanis, was so beautiful that she made the deity jealous. So, the goddess of the hunt acted on her envy by expelling Titanis and turning her into a doe.

There is a similar story about Athena. It is said that she was so jealous of the Gorgon Medusa's beauty that she turned her hair into snakes. Hera is similarly said to have given Antigone a head of serpents for boasting that she was more beautiful than the goddess.

Love

An example of a person transformed into an animal because a god was in love with them was the Argive princess Io, whom Zeus was infatuated with. Although the details of the various versions of her story differ, they all agree that she was turned into a cow because of this. One story says that Zeus transformed her to prevent Hera from discovering them. Another one has it that the girl did this herself to avoid the Olympian queen's wrath, and a third version mentions that the goddess transformed her mortal rival as a punishment. See Chapter 3 for more about Io.

Mortals and Heroes Who Transformed Themselves

A less common theme in Greek myth is mortals and heroes transforming themselves.

Io

As mentioned above, in one version of her story, Io turned herself into a cow to avoid the wrath of Hera. However, in other versions of this story, it was her lover or his wife who transformed her.

Glaucus

Glaucus was originally a mortal but achieved immortality by eating a magic herb. His fellow men refused to accept his new state, so he took to the water and became a sea god. Apollo allowed him to predict the future, so the human-turned-divinity would rise out of the ocean to warn sailors of coming disasters.

Animal and Plant Metamorphosis Stories

In many Ancient Greek myths, mortals are transformed into animals, usually by the gods. We explore a few examples below.

Animal Metamorphosis

Arachne

Arachne, a girl from Lydia, was known for her talent for weaving. One day, she bragged that she was a better weaver than Athena, so the goddess challenged her. On the tapestry she entered into their competition, Arachne depicted various stories of gods seducing mortal women. This enraged her opponent and motivated her to beat the girl. Distraught, the mortal tried to hang herself, but Athena turned her into a spider instead. This meant that Arachne's life was spared, and she could continue pursuing her passion for spinning webs. Interestingly, the word *arákhnē* is also Greek for "spider," meaning she gave her name to the creature she was transformed into.

Dionysus's Nurses

In a story recorded by the poet Pseudo-Oppian, Dionysus is said to have transformed his childhood nurses into leopards when they asked him to. They wanted him to do this so that they could tear apart Pentheus, the king of Thebes who had tried to outlaw their worship of the god they were tending to.

Hecuba

Hecuba was the wife of King Priam of Troy. When the city fell, she was given as a prize to Odysseus. When the Greek party was stationed at Thrace, the goddess Hecate took pity on the former queen and transformed her into a dog, allowing her to run away and escape from her captors.

The Tyrrhenian Pirates

One story tells that the god Dionysus took the form of a young man and began wandering Earth. When he was near the sea, some Tyrrhenian pirates saw and kidnapped him, unaware that he was a god.

The men intended to sell him into slavery or sexually assault him, but, as they were tying him up, the ship's captain, Acoetes, realized that something was wrong and that the individual they had abducted was not a fellow human but a divine being. In vain, he tried to stop his crewmates.

Eventually, Dionysus revealed his true identity to his captors—the names of whom were Aethalides, Alcimedon, Dictys, Epopeus, Libys, Lycabas, Melas, Medon, Opheltes, and Simon—by filling the ship with beasts and vines. Terrified, they abandoned the vessel and dived into the sea. As they did so, they were transformed into dolphins. The only one spared was Acoetes.

Plant Metamorphosis

Many women are transformed into plants in Greek myth as a means of either escaping sexual advances or punishment. Let's take a look at some of these stories.

Philyra

The story of Philyra involves multiple transformations. An ancient tradition says that Cronus, the father of the Olympian gods, also fathered the centaur Chiron with an Oceanid nymph, Philyra. Her son was born half-man, half-horse because the Titan had turned himself into a stallion to mate with her. In turn, she had turned herself into a mare to escape his advances.

Another tradition says that Philyra was so shocked by the appearance of her child that she prayed to Zeus to transform her, so he turned her into a linden tree, which has the name *phylira* in Greek.

Phylira's story is comparable to that of the nymph and follower of Artemis, Callisto, who Hera transformed into a bear as a punishment for having a son, Arcas, with Zeus (see Chapter 3).

Myrrha

As you may recall from Chapter 3, the gods transformed Myrrha into a tree to protect her from punishment for having an affair with her father, the Assyrian king, Theiras. She was also the mother of the handsome Adonis, whom Aphrodite and Persephone fought over.

Daphne

Eros, the god of love, and Apollo, the god of music and poetry, argued when the latter teased the former about his archery skills. Eros retaliated by making his rival fall in love with Daphne, a beautiful naiad said to be the daughter of the Ladon River.

Apollo chased the nymph, and she ran toward the mountains to escape him. He was catching up with her, so she begged her father to help her turn into something else before her pursuer could reach her. Daphne was transformed into a laurel tree just in time to preserve her chastity. The laurel has been Apollo's sacred tree ever since.

Not all plant transformation stories involve women escaping from men or the consequences of being seduced. One example is that of Narcissus, who gave his name to the flower.

Narcissus

Narcissus was so handsome that he fell in love with his reflection and did nothing but stare at it all day. This caused him to neglect the nymph, Echo, who had fallen in love with him, causing her to pine away and die. As for the object of her affection, some stories say he was killed as a punishment for neglecting Echo. Others say he was unable to leave his reflection, so he eventually withered away and died of starvation and thirst. It is said that either his corpse or the blood from a self-inflicted stab wound turned into the flowers named after him, giving him a form of immortality.

Other Categories of Transformation

Many different kinds of transformation or metamorphosis take place in Greek myth. Some of these involve changing sexes or changing an inanimate object into a person or the other way around. Here are some examples.

Caenis/Caeneus

Caenis, as she was called in her feminine form, was a woman who either had consensual sex or was raped by the sea god Poseidon. She responded to this event by asking him to change her into a strong, formidable man. He granted her wish, and she went on to be the hero known as Caeneus.

In Greek, "Caenis" means "new," implying that Poseidon gave the hero a new identity.

In other stories, individuals are transformed into the opposite sex as a punishment. Some examples are that of Siproites and Tiresias.

Siproites

Siproites was a hunter from Crete who caught Artemis bathing naked. The goddess responded by turning him into a woman. Other accounts suggest that he attempted to rape her, thereby explaining why she felt the need to take such extreme measures (Obradovic, 2020).

Tiresias

One day, the prophet Tiresias came upon two snakes making love and hit the pair with his stick to separate them. Hera was angry about his overly aggressive response to their natural urges and punished him by turning him into a woman. He then spent several years in this form until he again encountered mating serpents. This time, he either left them alone or trampled them. Because he responded differently on this occasion, Tiresias became a man once more.

Galatea

Galatea was a statue of womanly perfection that the sculptor Pygmalion created. He had become disillusioned with women, but he fell in love with his creation, so Aphrodite turned her into a real woman so that he could marry her. See Chapter 8 for more about the pair.

Arsinoë

Gods often turned mortals into statues as a punishment. One example is the story of the princess Arsinoë. She was courted by Arceophon, but her father Nicocreon disapproved and forbade them from marrying. The young man still tried to see her behind her father's back, bribing her wet nurse to let him meet the princess. However, Arsinoë told her parents what he had done. They punished the nurse by maiming her and kicking her out of the palace, and the girl's suitor killed himself. When she leaned out of her window to watch his funeral procession go by, Aphrodite turned her into a stone statue as punishment for betraying the man who loved her.

A similar story is that of Anaxarete, who had attracted the attention of Iphis. She rejected his advances and mocked him until he took his own life, but the maiden did not feel guilty when he died. Instead, she made unflattering comments during his funeral, angering Aphrodite who turned her into stone.

For the opposite reason, others were turned into statutes in response to their grief. For example, Heracles's mother, Alcmene, was turned into stone after the death of her son.

Summary

Transformations and metamorphoses happen for many reasons in Greek myth. The gods usually turned mortals into new forms, either as a punishment or to protect them. Other times, it's the result of a human who wants to end their life so that they might live on in another way. In this way, an ending becomes a beginning. In other instances, the transformation is a reward or is self-inflicted.

Greek myth often explores the deeper side of human nature. This is demonstrated by the exploration of shape-shifting in the myths above, and it's expanded on in the next chapter, where we look at how Greek myth has influenced modern psychology and the psychological understandings we can derive from these stories.

CHAPTER 8
MYTHOLOGY OF THE MIND:
ARCHETYPES AND PSYCHOLOGY

Educating the mind without educating the heart is no education at all.

– Aristotle

Greek mythology is full of stories with moral meaning or those that tell us something about human nature. For this reason, some of these, such as the myths of Oedipus and Electra, have formed the basis of modern psychological theories. The canon also provides us with examples of common archetypes we might encounter, both in life and fiction. We will explore some examples in this chapter.

Jungian Archetypes in Greek Mythology

Greek mythology is full of archetypes. In this context, the term often refers to recurring patterns or stereotypes. The psychologist Carl Jung suggested that these common characteristics (or patterns of behavior or personality prototypes) influence our lives in various ways. This idea originates in

Plato's writings from the fourth century B.C.E. He described this phenomenon as *eidos*, a form or idea.

Borda (2023) describes archetypes as:

> The universal principles, patterns, and powers that move us all and shape our lives from the collective unconscious—the containing psychological matrix underlying consciousness. They are the governing principles in the background of experience that together comprise a kind of thematic framework within which our lives unfold. The archetypes manifest within and through our thoughts and feelings, drives and desires, and through circumstances and events in the world. They are not causes in the usual sense, but they are enacted by and revealed through causal chains of events.

Jung focused on four foundational archetypes: the shadow, anima, animus, and the self. He understood Greek myths and symbols as expressions, and, thus, reflections, of the psyche. Some examples include the figures of the hero, the mother, the child, the trickster, the spirit (one example being the wise old man), rebirth, and Dionysus—who represented the full range of human emotions. Today, these archetypes manifest as categories such as the wise sage, the young innocent, the explorer, the rebel, the hero, the lover, the caregiver, and so forth. Hence, these recurring characters help us understand ourselves and others around us.

Freudian Interpretations of Greek Myth: Oedipus and Electra

In the early 1900s, the psychoanalyst Sigmund Freud used the stories of Oedipus and Electra to explore his theory of psychosexual stages of development. He believed that in the phallic stage of development, in which children self-discover their body parts and form a connection with pleasure, the child comes to identify and love the parent of the opposite sex and feels hostility toward the other parent.

The Oedipus Complex

In Greek mythology, Oedipus is famous for killing his father and marrying his mother. When he was born, an oracle forecasted that he would kill King Laius of Thebes, and wed his mother, Queen Jocasta. To prevent the prophecy from being fulfilled, Laius exposed his son and left him to die.

However, Oedipus was rescued, and, years later, he unknowingly killed his father and married Jocasta. When she discovered that her new husband was her long-lost son, she killed herself; meanwhile, Oedipus was so horrified by his actions that he blinded himself and went into exile with his daughters Antigone and Ismene.

According to Freud's theory, the Oedipus complex occurs when a boy aged between three and six years old becomes sexually attracted to his mother and hostile toward his father, whom he views as a rival. This is an unconscious part of development, and the resulting conflict comes about because the boy develops pleasurable desires for his mother.

Due to his newfound attraction to his female parent, the boy directs envy and jealousy at his father, who stands in his way of receiving her attention and affection. These strong feelings toward both parents lead to him fantasizing about getting rid of the male parent and taking his place. Freud proposes that, as a consequence of the child's hostility, he experiences castration anxiety, an irrational fear that his father will remove his penis as a punishment.

The solution to the complex occurs once boys begin to identify with their same-sex parents. As they start to see themselves in their fathers, they come to internalize the values, behaviors, and attitudes they witness, leading to the development of a masculine gender identity, which eventually resolves the internal conflict. The father transforms into a role model as opposed to a rival. By identifying with the former aggressor, boys acquire their superego and the male sex role while substituting their desire for their mother with their desire for other women (Mcleod, 2024).

The Electra Complex

Electra is another Greek mythological figure. Along with her brother Orestes, she is remembered for plotting the death of her mother, Clytemnestra, and stepfather, Aegisthus. Their scheme was a revenge plot for the murder of the siblings' father, Agamemnon (Bell, 1991).

The term "Electra complex" describes the female version of the Oedipus complex. Similarly to the latter, it involves a girl aged between three and six becoming unconsciously sexually attached to her father and increasingly hostile toward her mother. The concept is usually attributed to Freud but was proposed by his protégé, Carl Jung (Jung & Kerenyi, 1963).

The Electra complex begins with the child believing she has been castrated because she is missing male genitalia, leading to penis envy. She blames her mother for this. Like boys with their fathers, for girls to develop their female sex role and superego, they need to identify with their parent of the same sex. However, there is no motivation to give up the father as a love object in favor of this identification, so it is less conclusively resolved than its Oedipal counterpart. Consequently, at least, according to this theory, the female superego is weaker, and women's identities as separate, independent persons are less developed than men's.

Lessons About Personal Growth From Greek Mythology

There are plenty of lessons about personal growth in Greek mythology. We explore some of these below.

Narcissus and Echo:
The Perils of Self-Love and Codependency

The nymph Echo was a follower of Zeus's wife, Hera, whom she annoyed by gossiping about the king of the gods' love affairs. To punish her, the goddess took away Echo's ability to speak for herself, so she could only repeat the words of others.

So, when she fell in love with the handsome Narcissus, she could not tell him. Meanwhile, the object of her affection would only stare at his beautiful reflection, as he was so impossibly attractive that he had fallen in love with his image reflected in a pool of water. Heartbroken that her love was unrequited, Echo yearns for him in sorrow among the rocks (Wilkinson, 1998; Cartwright, 2023).

In one version of the story, as a punishment for his neglect of the nymph, Narcissus is killed. In another, he is unable to tear himself away from his reflection, so he pines away in despair until he finally dies of starvation and thirst. However, he achieved immortality of a kind when either his corpse or the blood from a self-inflicted stab wound turned into flowers that bore his name, as we saw in Chapter 7.

Today, his name has become synonymous with those who are obsessed with their own appearance, status, or finding perfect love. The story of the relationship between the two mythological figures is also typical of the intimate relationships of people diagnosed with narcissistic personality disorder.

Because such egocentric individuals are self-absorbed and focus on themselves and their desires, they often attract codependent partners like Echo. Whereas Narcissus is overly infatuated with himself, she is too focused on pleasing him. She is therefore representative of someone who sacrifices their needs to accommodate others. Like her, the partners of narcissists often idolize them, don't advocate for themselves, and feel guilty if they do try to assert their wants and needs (Lancer, 2017).

In extreme cases, like Echo, being unable to advocate for individual wants and needs in a relationship can lead codependents to fade away.

Pygmalion and Galatea: Projecting Ideals Onto Partners

Pygmalion was a sculptor who had become disillusioned with women due to the low morals of some of those he had encountered. This led him to decide to reject their company. Instead, he tried to create the perfect woman.

Eventually, he created a beautiful sculpture out of ivory, which he named Galatea. He was so moved by the perfection of his statue that he became obsessed with it and fell in love with it. He began calling it his wife, brought it gifts, kissed and caressed it, and talked to it every day. He brought Galatea offerings he thought women would like, such as beads, pretty seashells, baubles, songbirds, and flowers. He would dress the ivory woman in nice clothes and put rings on her fingers, necklaces around her neck, and attach earrings to her ears.

Eventually, at a festival in honor of Aphrodite, Pygmalion begged the goddess of love to give him a wife like his creation. The goddess listened and granted his wish. When he returned home, he realized Galatea was becoming more and more alive as he touched her. Soon, she had been transformed from stone into a mortal woman. Aphrodite herself then married the couple (Chaliakopoulos, 2021).

It has been suggested that he used his skills as a sculptor to correct the flaws he perceived in flesh and blood women. Nevertheless, Pygmalion's story is ironic, as his masterpiece was still a statue representation of the women he had sworn to reject.

Pygmalion's story may also be an example of the psychological concept of projection. This is the process of a person displacing their feelings onto another human, animal, or object. The term is often a defensive reaction, where the individual blames their unacceptable urges or another behavior on another. For example, if a bully ridicules a shy peer, they may be casting their low self-esteem onto their victim. We also make emotional assumptions about others based on a hidden bias in our lived experience.

The commonly known Pygmalion effect is related to psychological projection, as it is a phenomenon where higher expectations lead to improved performance in others. Its mythological namesake's story tells of how a sculptor's great expectations led to his work coming to life. Based on this interpretation, this story teaches leaders to expect more from others and encourages followers to perform better (Perera, 2024).

However, the Pygmalion effect could also relate to the more common understanding of psychological projection, as the act of projecting perfection on Galatea may prove disappointing to the sculptor when he realizes that, as a human, she is imperfect—not a flawless statue.

Midas: The Corrupting Influence of Greed

Midas, famous for his greed, was a king of Phrygia and is sometimes said to be the son of the goddess Cybele.

One well-known story about Midas is that of the golden touch. According to this tale, some peasants brought the drunken satyr, Silenus, in chains, to the king. Recognizing the part-beast, part-man as a companion of Dionysus, Midas returned him to Mount Olympus. As a reward, the god of revelry granted him a wish, so he requested that anything he touched would turn to gold.

Midas immediately tested his new power. He pulled a twig from a holm oak and, much to his surprise, it turned into gold. He then lifted a stone, which did the same. He also transformed some grain, apples, and wheat. By the time he returned to his palace, he was leaving golden door handles behind him.

But his good fortune failed when *everything* Midas touched was transformed, including his food and wine, so he could not eat or drink. One version of the story says that he even turned one of his daughters into a statue by mistake (Chaliakopoulos, 2024).

Midas begged the gods to end his torment and was told to wash in the Pactolus River, in modern-day Turkey, where, ever since, visitors have found grains of gold.

Midas wished everything he came into contact with would become a source of wealth, but he soon realized that this was not a blessing but a curse. He was the richest man alive, but he sought to become even wealthier. By asking Dionysus to satisfy his greed and make everything he laid his hands on turn to gold, he demonstrated his arrogance and obsession with excessive material prosperity (Chaliakopoulos, 2024). From a psychological perspective, the consequences King Midas faced encourage us to think and appreciate the consequences of becoming slaves to our desires.

Sisyphus and Tantalus: Symbols of Existential Angst

The Story of King Sisyphus

King Sisyphus of Corinth managed to cheat death when he told his wife he did not want a funeral after he died, which he knew would offend Hades. So, when he entered the land of the departed, the god sent him back to Earth for burial. But Sisyphus returned to his throne instead. When he later died again, as punishment, he was forced to roll a rock up a hill in the underworld forever.

In his philosophical essay titled "The Myth of Sisyphus" (1942), Albert Camus argues that humans are body-soul-spirit beings in a constant state of tension between an inner longing for meaningfulness and the lack thereof in the world. Difficulty finding a reason for being can lead to feelings of anxiety and despair, chronic apathy, and aimlessness.

In the essay, Camus addresses whether life is worth living in a world without purpose. He uses the story of Sisyphus to explore this, as the king is condemned to carry out an eternal punishment in which he must complete the same task over and over again. However, Camus sees a certain beauty and a sense of fulfillment in the struggle itself. He proposes that, although life is hopeless and absurd, it is up to the individual to find meaning and happiness despite that. He suggests that the mythical king is not tortured. Rather, he is happy, as he constantly makes an effort in a futile situation. Camus therefore uses Sisyphus's story as an example of how striving and pursuing personal goals provides us with meaning and fulfillment, regardless of the outcome of these efforts.

The Myth of King Tantalus

The gods punished King Tantalus, the ruler of Lydia in modern-day Turkey, for his bad deeds and for challenging their divinity. He doubted that the gods were all-powerful and all-knowing, so he invited them to a banquet and served up Pelops, his son, to test whether they would know what they were eating. Straight away, the divine guests realized what their host had done. They brought the prince back to life and sentenced his father to everlasting thirst and hunger in Tartarus, the deepest region of the underworld.

The story of King Tantalus could also be seen as an example of existential angst. Unlike Sisyphus, his divine punishment was unlikely to bring him any satisfaction. However, Tantalus's anxiety about life's meaning was expressed through his doubt of the divinity of the gods. This led him to behave in dangerous, destructive, and immoral ways until the deities proved their power and punished him for his skepticism.

Summary

As we have seen, Greek mythology is full of stories of personal growth and examples of how our behavior can have a positive or negative impact on the people around us. It has also been applied to explain developmental stages or unusual behavior in psychology.

Furthermore, this chapter has shown that these myths can be seen as metaphors for personal growth and the necessity of recognizing the fluidity of identity, reminding us that life is an inevitable series of constant changes. The ancient Greeks recognized the symbolic and literal transformations that shape our world, and the tales offer insights into the human experience and the forces that govern it.

In this sense, Greek mythology is full of wisdom, something explored in greater depth in the next chapter.

CHAPTER 9

MYTHOLOGY MEETS PHILOSOPHY:

WISDOM OF THE ANCIENT GREEKS

The only true wisdom is in knowing you know nothing.

– Socrates

Greek myths were not just told for fun. They were also told to transmit social ideals and wisdom from one generation to the next. From these stories, we know that divine justice and cosmic order formed an important part of the Greek religion, and a prime indicator of this is the prominence of the goddess of justice, divine order, law, and custom—Themis, one of the Titans and the second wife of Zeus.

Intriguingly, texts such as the *Iliad* and the *Odyssey* tell us that, for the Greeks, concepts like justice were socially constructed, both on divine and human plains. On both levels, there was a hierarchy of power and a structure of authority, which helped order the cosmos and ensured that the appropriate action took place.

Below, we look at how philosophy shaped ancient and modern understandings of Greek myth and explore some examples of the moral messages and wisdom found in these tales.

Relevance of Myth to Stoicism, Cynicism, and Other Greek Philosophical Schools

Mythology was regularly discussed by the Greek philosophical schools, which came about in the sixth century B.C.E., long after myths came into circulation. These groups aimed to make sense of the world using reason. We will explore the relevance of these tales to two of them, Stoicism and Cynicism.

According to the tenets of Stoicism, founded in around 300 B.C.E., human beings naturally aim to secure success for themselves and live in harmony with others. The philosophy therefore encourages individuals to find a balance between these two competing desires. So, for example, Stoics believed that it was acceptable to wish for wealth, provided that desire did not go against an individual's commitment to their ethics. They also believed it was acceptable to live within the confines of societal expectations, as long as those were just and did not diminish personal virtue (Rattray, 2021).

Founded in the fifth century B.C.E., Cynicism was a philosophy where followers denounced luxury and wealth in favor of simpler pleasures. Thus, unlike the Stoics, the Cynics placed greater value on the nature of the individual, personal freedom, and self-sufficiency. They strove to free themselves from the perceived burdens of materialism, so they rejected social conventions, including wealth and home comforts.

In ancient Greece, they were known as *kunikos* (meaning "dog-like"), as many who followed the philosophy lived on the streets like stray animals, with some surviving on what they received from begging alone. By opting to stand apart from societal systems, the Cynics recognized how those systems can lead us away from living according to our true nature and experiencing authentic freedom and happiness.

The main difference between the two factions is that the Stoics believed that a good life could be achieved within the confines of human desires and societal expectations; meanwhile, the Cynics felt that true happiness could only be achieved if the individual freed themselves from all limitations, including those imposed by internal wants or by others (Rattray, 2021).

Both schools of thought also had divergent understandings of Greek myth. The Stoics regarded the cosmos as a structure formed and guided by Logos, the controlling principle of all things. Accordingly, they thought that it must be amenable to reason. While myths often seemed less than rational, philosophers could not simply dismiss them because the stories had the authority of time-honored poets like Homer and Hesiod. So, the Stoics understood the myths allegorically. This meant that they saw them as tales infused with life lessons and moral meanings. Thus, they rationalized the mythological tradition.

The most famous of the Cynics was Diogenes of Sinope, known as Diogenes the Dog due to his radical behavior, including public defecation (Bell, 2022). He used Greek myth to rationalize his behavior, understanding the pursuits of mankind in a Sisyphean manner. To him, just as the subject of the myth carried the boulder up the mountain every day only to have it roll back down again, man's pursuit of wealth and power was equally meaningless. Therefore, as Stoicism had, Cynicism saw Greek mythology as allegory rather than literal truth.

Plato's Dialogues and Mythological Allegories

Stoicism and Cynicism were not the only philosophical schools to consider the role of myth. The philosopher Plato (ca. 427–348 B.C.E.) also used it to illustrate his thinking. Unlike some of his counterparts, his works do not contain dry analytical arguments. Instead, he used lively fictional or semi-fictional dialogues to illustrate his points. This device makes his work some of the most appealing and interesting philosophical texts ever written and means that they continue to resonate with modern audiences.

Plato weaved myths, allegories, and metaphors into his writing. One example is when he compared the soul (or the human mind or psyche) to a charioteer being pulled by two winged horses, one of which was tame and noble, representing reason, and the other embodying passion in its wildness and unruliness (Burton, 2022).

Plato also used both traditional myths and those he invented to illustrate his points. One of his famous fictionalizations was the story of Atlantis, which served as a representation of the philosopher's vision of an ideal society.

In *Timaeus and Critias* (ca. 360 B.C.E.), Plato tells us that Atlantis was a large island, bigger than Libya and Asia combined, and located in the

Atlantic Ocean, where it was ruled over by a powerful and remarkable dynasty of kings who were directly descended from Poseidon. However, this lineage eventually became diluted through mixing with mortal stock.

The degeneration of the dynasty and, by extension, the noble civilization, led to a war with its former ally, Athens. It was this conflict that led to Atlantis's destruction, which Plato says took place 9,000 years previously. He states (Stewart, 2011):

> Sometime later, there were earthquakes and floods of extraordinary violence, and in a single dreadful day and night all your life [i.e., Athenian] fighting men were swallowed up by the earth, and the island of Atlantis was similarly swallowed up by the sea and vanished.

Thus, Plato invented the myth of this island to demonstrate how the degeneration of a dynasty might lead to the destruction of a civilization. This shows us that, for him, myths could be used to prove a point and illustrate philosophical concepts.

Lessons on Life, Love, and Wisdom in Greek Mythology

Greek mythology is full of moral lessons and ethical quandaries. We consider some examples of these below.

Icarus: Balancing Ambition and Caution

Icarus was the son of the inventor Daedalus, who built the labyrinth that housed the Minotaur and Naucrate, one of King Minos's slaves. The king imprisoned him and his father after the inventor had displeased him, as mentioned in Chapter 2.

Daedalus eventually planned an ingenious escape after watching sea birds fly overhead the tower that he and his son were locked away in. Inspired, he made wings for himself and Icarus out of feathers and wax. They planned to fly over the ocean to find a new home and freedom (Padian, 2024).

Before they took to the sky, Daedalus told his son not to fly too high or close to the sun or too low or near the sea, as either extreme could be dangerous and kill him. However, Icarus ignored his father's warnings. Intoxicated by the thrill of the flight, he soared higher and higher. When he got too close to the sun, the wax that bound his wings began to melt, and he plummeted to his death into the sea as his father watched in horror.

This story teaches us to be wary of hubris—the excessive pride that makes us unable to see our limitations. The tragedy of Icarus is that he pursued his desires and ignored the dangerous consequences of his decisions. His actions were coupled with exaggerated self-confidence, as it was because of this that he felt he could overcome the limits of his man-made wings.

The two characters represent the challenge we all face of maintaining the delicate balance between our greatest desires and the limitations nature and mortality impose. Daedalus is cautious and understands the restrictions around him while Icarus is blinded by his pride and ambition to push the boundaries of what is humanly possible. He also represents the inherent risk connected with pursuing progress, discovery, and knowledge. Their story encourages us to reflect on our ambitions and the confines of reality, which tells us that we must navigate life with self-awareness, prudence, and humility.

Baucis and Philemon: The Blessings of Hospitality

One day, Zeus and Hermes decided to visit Earth because they wanted to observe humanity and see how its people lived. They came to the mortal realm disguised as poor travelers because they did not want anyone to know who they were. However, most people they encountered were unkind to them, turned them away from their homes, and refused them food and shelter.

Eventually, in Phrygia, the gods came across a shabby hut with a roof of thatch and weeds where Baucis and Philemon, a hospitable elderly couple, lived. They had little, but they were content because they had enough. They welcomed the men, and their kindness made up for their lack of material comforts. They found a little honey to go with the simple meal they prepared and gave their guests the bit of wine they had.

Soon, though, Baucis and Philemon noticed that there was something different about the travelers, as the flow of wine never diminished. They realized that the men were more than mortals and were ashamed they had so little to offer them. So, they decided to kill the goose who guarded their home, but he was too fast for them, and they couldn't catch and kill him.

Zeus and Hermes were touched by the goodness of the old couple and declared themselves. They asked their hosts to accompany them to a summit on a little hill. There, Baucis and Philemon saw all the land, apart from their humble home, flooded and destroyed. The gods then transformed their hosts' ramshackle house into a temple.

Zeus asked Baucis and Philemon what he could do to please them the most. They requested to serve him and guard his shrine. The couple also asked never to be separated from each other in life or death. So, they were installed at the temple and lived out their days in contentment. Eventually, they died together in perfect peace. Philemon was transformed into an oak and Baucis a linden tree. Their boughs were intertwined, so they remained together forever.

The story of the couple tells us that, however poor we are, we have it in us to help others. Their example teaches us that contentment is found in small things, not worldly greed or ambition.

Prometheus: The Perils and Promise of Foresight

Prometheus's name means "the foreseeing" (Stapleton, 1986). He was known to have a unique ability to see what he would do ahead of time and the likely consequences of his and others' decisions. Some of his best-known actions were forming the first man out of clay, according to one myth, and stealing fire from Mount Olympus. Both acts showed that he had the foresight to create man and to look after his creation. In Chapter 5, we looked at both of the above stories as well as his punishment and torture on Mount Caucasus.

Zeus was motivated to this extreme measure because of the Titan's foresight, demonstrating the perils he faced because of his ability to predict the future. In that instance, Prometheus knew that Thetis, a Nereid, would give birth to a son destined to be greater than his father. As both Zeus and his brother Poseidon were attracted to the nymph, there was a real risk that she could have a divine son who would grow up to challenge Zeus's position as king of the gods. Prometheus's torture continued until Heracles rescued him, and he then shared this secret gained through foresight.

The character of Prometheus, who teaches us the importance of thinking ahead, is a direct contrast to his brother, Epimetheus. His twin, whose name means "afterthought," was known for being foolish, and he is best remembered as the husband of Pandora.

In Hesiod's version of the myth, Epimetheus is so named not because he cannot see the future but because he does not remember, at a critical moment in the present, what he has been told in the past. His tendency not to think ahead leads Pandora, whom Zeus created to bring strife to humanity, to come to Earth as his wife. It is said that (Atwill, 1998: 118):

> Epimetheus did not think about what Prometheus had said to him, bidding him never to take a gift of Olympian Zeus, but to send it back for fear it might prove to be something harmful to men. But he took the gift, and afterward, when the evil thing was already his, he understood.

The suggestion throughout the narrative is that Epimetheus's failure to remember his brother's warning about Olympian gifts is what brought about a new dimension to human suffering. The promise of foresight and what makes it important is its use for preventing adverse situations and outcomes. Thus, in the case of Pandora, it fails.

Summary

Greek myth was not always part of a clear-cut belief system. Often, the stories were moral and individual examples of how to live better and to tell audiences what values were important to exhibit in daily life.

The intersection of Greek mythology and philosophy explored concepts of divine justice, cosmic order, and ethical quandaries. Ancient Greek myths tended to depict a universe governed by an intricate balance of order and chaos, where the actions of gods and mortals alike are subject to overarching cosmic principles.

Philosophers like Plato and Aristotle drew on these myths to investigate notions of the ideal society, divine justice, what constitutes ethical behavior, individual conscience, and the consequences of moral and immoral actions. Greek philosophical ideas still influence contemporary reflections on ethics, justice, and the human condition.

In the next chapter, we move on from philosophy to the universal meanings and motifs found in Greek mythology.

Chapter 10

Comparative Mythology:

Universal Themes and Motifs

Captive Greece captured, in turn, her uncivilized conquerors, and brought the arts to rustic Latium.

– Roman poet Horace, writing in the first century B.C.E.

Greek mythology does not exist in isolation—it also parallels other ancient mythological canons including those of the Romans, the Vikings, and the Celts. We explore some of these similarities and present the universal themes of mythology below.

Similarities and Differences to Roman Mythology and the Etruscan Pantheon

The Romans conquered Greece over the course of a century. The process began after the Greek defeats by Roman forces at the Battle of Corinth in 146 B.C.E and the Battle of Pydna in 168 B.C.E., respectively. Roman occupation of Greece was then formally established after the Battle of Actium in 31 B.C.E when Augustus defeated the Greek queen of Egypt, Cleopatra VII, and her lover, the Roman general, Mark Antony. After this, he took Alexandria, the last city of Hellenistic Egypt, in 30 B.C.E. (Ferguson, 2024). The conquest allowed for Greek culture, including religion, to be transmitted to the conquerors.

However, there is evidence that suggests that Greek cultural influence dictated the direction of Roman religion from a far earlier date. The Etruscans, another civilization of ancient Italy, who had preceded the Romans and were eventually assimilated into their way of life, had worshipped many Greek gods and also sought to purchase and imitate its art. Influenced by their forbears, the Romans adapted the iconography and mythology of many Greek gods and goddesses to suit their purposes, thereby using these characters and their stories to create a new tradition inspired by Greek myth (Lesso, 2022b).

Similarities

The Greek and Roman religions were so similar due to their close cultural connections. As the Roman Republic grew and acquired Greek territories, it also adopted and adapted different aspects of the existing culture to suit its citizens.

The mythologies of both civilizations were inherently similar, as both focused on the relationships between gods and mortals and tried to make sense of a chaotic universe. In both instances, myths tackled important topics ranging from the world's creation to what happens after death. Furthermore, both mythologies served the purpose of retelling important historical events so that people would remember their ancestors and their wars, triumphs, and failures.

The gods and goddesses of Greek culture also greatly influenced the creation of Roman deities and mythology. Most of the gods in the latter pantheon served as renamed counterparts to Greek divinities and had similar titles or powers. The respective deities also had human qualities, making them relatable to the people telling and hearing stories of their exploits. A list of Greek gods and their Roman parallels is presented below.

Greek name	Roman name	Role
Zeus	Jupiter	King of the gods
Hera	Juno	Queen of the gods
Aphrodite	Venus	Goddess of love and beauty
Ares	Mars	God of war
Artemis	Diana	Goddess of hunting, animals, and childbirth
Athena	Minerva	Goddess of wisdom and defense
Dionysus	Bacchus	God of war, pleasure, and destroy
Hades	Pluto	God of the underworld
Poseidon	Neptune	God of the seas

Differences

However, the Romans did not simply inherit Greek mythology and claim it as their own. Instead, they were active interpreters of the myths and culture. Notably, Greek and Roman mythology were told and distributed in different ways. While the former contained compelling tales of gods and goddesses and heroes and monsters that were orally transmitted, the latter was written in prose and grounded in history and institutions.

Other differences between the two mythologies include:

Personality Traits

There are significant differences between the personality traits of the gods and goddesses. Greek deities tended to possess admirable qualities such as heroism, boldness, strength, and intelligence. They often also had flaws that led to their downfalls, like pride, cruelty, and blind ambition. In contrast, Roman gods were less individualistic, more singular in purpose, and focused on serving and protecting family and state.

Physical Characteristics

Greek mythology placed far more emphasis on beauty and physical appearance than its Roman counterpart. The bodies of certain Greek gods were described as powerful, beautiful, and strong while ugly characters were presented as terrifying and tormented monsters, such as Medusa. On the other hand, in Roman mythology, the physical appearance of the god was rarely commented on, leaving it to the listener or reader to imagine for themselves.

Opinion of Mortals

The Greeks viewed gods as higher beings whose status was holy and unattainable by mortals. The expectation was that humans would contribute positively to society and honor the deities during their brief time on Earth. However, the Romans believed that people should aspire to live like the gods and goddesses they worshipped. These contrasting ideas were reflected in the different ways they told the stories of divine beings.

Origin Stories

The creation of the universe is one of the foundational stories of Greek mythology— you can see Chapter 5 for more details. However, the Roman account ignores the creation of the universe and instead focuses on the foundation of Rome. Here, the twins Romulus and Remus were said to be predestined to be the founders of the city. Many Roman authors recorded this story, including Virgil. It was believed that the brothers were descended from the hero Aeneas, a Trojan hero, and were the sons of Mars, the god of war.

Despite this difference, there is a parallel in Greek mythology in terms of its focus on the overthrow of the Titans by the Olympians, who came to be the gods and goddesses mainly worshipped by the ancient Greeks.

The Afterlife

The Greeks did not consider the afterlife to be of much importance, as they emphasized that humans were remembered and rewarded for the good deeds they performed in the mortal realm. Homer portrayed the underworld in the *Odyssey*, but it is presented as a bleak place for all the dead that reside there rather than a punishment for those who were evil in life.

The afterlife is seen in a very different way in Roman mythology. After death, mortals were transformed and allowed to live among the gods. Ancient Romans also believed that after they died, they would be worshipped by the state and family members and could intervene and provide guidance to the living.

Other Mythic Parallels

There are also similarities between Greek myth and other ancient traditions. Here are some examples.

Comparing Greek Myths to Norse and Celtic Mythology

As with Greek and Roman mythology, the Norse and Celtic mythical canons also included a comprehensive pantheon of gods and goddesses with human qualities that made them relatable to the people who worshipped them.

Norse Mythology

Norse mythology presents its head god in a similar way to how Greek mythology portrays Zeus in the sense that Odin, king of Asgard, was the chief of the divine beings. However, this is where the similarity ends, as these figures are quite different from one another. Although there is alignment in the roles Odin and Zeus played in their respective cosmos, they were very different in terms of what powers they possessed and the factors they represented.

Odin was associated with healing, sorcery, death, and battle; meanwhile, Zeus was the lord of the sky and lightning, and he had complete control over what happened in this region. A closer comparison in Norse mythology is Thor, the son of Odin and the god of thunder and lightning. There is no direct Greek parallel to Odin. Rather, different gods represent various powers he possessed. Apollo was the Greek god of medicine, while Hades was the god of death and was the goddess Hecate of sorcery. Athena and Ares ruled over battle.

In Greek mythology, the dead went to various parts of the underworld. Meanwhile, in Norse mythology, what happened to departed souls was not the domain of one god but depended on how the individual had met their end and which deity that came under. For example, those who died in combat might be sent to the realm of Folkvangr, presided over by Freyja, the goddess of love and sexuality as well as battle and death. Alternatively, the Valkyries may have recruited them and sent them to Valhalla, which was presided over by Odin (Mehrotra, 2016). In this sense, both traditions had separate, divergent understandings of what happened after death.

Celtic Mythology

There are some similarities between ancient Greek and Celtic myths. Notably, both contain plenty of monsters and mythical beasts, such as giants and centaurs. Other likenesses can be found in how each mythology treats heroes and the parallels between the afterlife in the Greek underworld and the Celtic otherworld.

Interestingly, both realms are located westward, over the great ocean. The Greek islands of Elysium are located in this direction, as are many of the magical islands of Irish Celtic myth, such as Mag Mell, Hy-Brasil, and Emain Ablach. Both are also said to be beneath the earth. Furthermore, as the Greeks did, the Celts thought that all the rivers of the world joined together as a "world river" that came from the otherworld by piercing out of the ground as springs of water.

There are also parallels between the Celtic hero Cú Chulainn and the most famous of all the Greek heroes, Heracles. The former was the superhero-like warrior of the *Ulster Cycle* stories. He was the son of the god Lugh, and he was associated with blacksmiths and craftsmen. He was Ulster's leading warrior and had a reputation as the lover of goddesses and the nemesis of a powerful female deity, The Morrígan. Although he performed many heroic deeds and sporting feats, he was also subject to the commands of his king and his gods. He died young, as is characteristic of the ideal Celtic warrior.

Both Cú Chulainn and Heracles are said to have traveled to distant lands and battled with many fantastical creatures on their adventures. However, unlike the Greek hero, Cú Chulainn is not responsible for conquering and taming the wild and chaotic forces of the world for the benefit of humanity. Instead, the *Ulster Cycle* depicts him as acting according to the interests of his liege lord in a similar way to Achilles in Greek myth. The young warrior may differ from Heracles in this aspect of his character because the Celtic myths were usually told at the courts of elite rulers, so they were designed to suit their value system rather than that of the common people.

Eastern Mythic Parallels

The ancient Greek religion was also similar to that of the ancient Near East. Parallels have been found between ancient Greek myths and those found in Sumerian, Babylonian, and Hittite cultures. In the past, such Eastern civilizations were dismissed by Western academics as "barbarian" or "pagan." However, more recent scholarship suggests that there were strong cultural connections between ancient Greece and its neighbors in this world region, as there are notable commonalities between the epics of Hesiod and Homer and those found in Mesopotamia and Egypt.

One example is a passage found in the opening of Homer's *Iliad*, in which Achilles proposes consulting with those experienced in divination to discover the cause of Apollo's anger after the god sent a plague to besiege the Greek camp. This is comparable to a passage in the prayers of the Hittite king Mursili II, who similarly asked to learn the reason for the divine wrath that had caused a pestilence in his country. In turn, this story was based on an older Sumerian original.

Another example is the Hittite myth titled the "Kingship in Heaven." This involves the violent severing of Heaven's penis, which reflects the story of Uranus's castration in Hesiod's *Theogony*. Additionally, the Hittite "Song of Ullikummi," where a weather god defeats another deity, is also reminiscent of how Zeus defeats Typhon in Hesiod's text (Noegel, 2006).

These examples thus suggest that the ancient poets Homer and Hesiod were inspired by the mythology of the cultures of the Near East. In this way, these stories made their way into Greek mythology in a similar way to how the Romans later adopted those of ancient Greece.

The Universal Motifs of Mythology

As mythology has informed people's worldview since the dawn of history, it is full of motifs and themes relating to the universality of the subjects it explores, from the creation of the world and civilization as we know it to what happens after we die.

Some examples of common threads found in world legends include war, flood, cyclical renewal, hubris, and fate versus free will. Perhaps the most significant is the hero's journey, which we explore below.

The Hero's Journey

Ancient Greek mythology marks the beginning of the narrative device known as "the hero's journey." This is a common template for stories, both myths and works of fiction, that involve a protagonist who goes on an adventure, wins in a decisive battle or crisis situation, and then returns home changed or transformed. It is seen in the *Odyssey* and the adventures of Heracles. The device is so well-established in literature that it has been divided into 12 key steps (Grammarly, 2023). These are:

1. **The call to adventure:** In the first step, the hero receives a message or has an encounter with an important figure who tells them to go on a quest and complete a mission.

2. **The refusal of the call:** The hero often initially refuses the summons due to fear, doubt, or a sense of inadequacy.

3. **Meeting the mentor:** A mentor provides the hero with support

and guidance on the path forward.

4. **Crossing the threshold:** The hero leaves the known world and travels into the unfamiliar. Here, they encounter tests, trials, and challenges.

5. **Allies, tests, and enemies:** With the aid of allies, the hero must overcome a series of obstacles and confrontations with their enemies.

6. **The approach to the innermost cave:** This is the location where the hero faces their greatest challenges and fears.

7. **The ordeal:** There is always a major obstacle or enemy that the hero must overcome to complete their journey.

8. **The reward:** The hero will then gain a reward, such as knowledge, insight, or a powerful object, to help them progress.

9. **The road back:** With the mission complete, the hero must travel back, facing new challenges and obstacles along the way.

10. **The resurrection:** The hero experiences a moment of death and rebirth, often conceptualized as a physical or metaphysical transformation.

11. **The return:** The changed hero eventually returns home and uses their new knowledge to benefit those around them.

12. **The freedom to live:** The hero's journey ends with the achievement of freedom and enlightenment.

Summary

This comparison of Greek mythology to other ancient mythological canons shows that there are some parallels between various belief systems. It is also apparent that Greek myths are full of some of the common tropes found throughout all narratives of this kind.

Several common motifs can be found in most major world mythologies. The recurrence of war and floods reflects humanity's desire for an explanation of natural disasters, such as that they are the result of divine retribution. Pride is another theme that makes an appearance across cultures, and it is a warning of overreaching ambition at the expense of consideration for our fellow humans. It is also a reminder of the need for humility. The universality of the conflict between free will and fate reflects the human need to explain or understand the balance between destiny and individual agency. This raises questions about the extent to which humans control our paths.

By comparing these mythological systems, this chapter has revealed how different cultures address similar existential questions and moral dilemmas, demonstrating the shared human quest to understand the world and our place within it.

We follow up this discussion by exploring how Greek mythology has influenced modern culture.

Chapter 11

The Muses' Legacy:

How Greek Mythology Continues to Shape Our World

The nine Greek Muses awakened again for this generation of man and meant to inspire mankind forward in the sciences and the arts.

– Lisa Kessler

Ever since Greek mythology was originally recorded by bards such as Homer and Hesiod, it has constantly been retold and adapted to meet the changing needs and preconceptions of different audiences. First, many myths were dramatized by ancient playwrights such as Aeschylus, Sophocles, and Euripides. They were then retold by Roman poets such as Ovid and Virgil. When they were rediscovered in the Renaissance and Neoclassical periods, they were rendered again in the paintings and sculptures of artists such as Botticelli and Bouguereau.

Here, we look at how these myths have been readapted in more recent times and how they continue to shape our world.

Modern Adaptations of Greek Myths

Below, we look at some examples of modern novels, poems, and plays that have adapted Greek myths for contemporary audiences.

Ulysses

One of the most famous adaptations of Greek myth in a modern novel is James Joyce's reimagining of Homer's epic poem the *Odyssey* in his novel *Ulysses* (1922).

Ulysses, a Latinized version of the name Odysseus, the hero of Homer's work, is made up of 18 episodes that roughly relate to the episodes in the *Odyssey*. The original poem chronicles how the Greek hero of the Trojan War spent 10 years trying to make his way back from Troy to his home on the island of Ithaca. However, while Homer describes plenty of violent storms, shipwrecks, and dramatic trials such as confrontations with giants, battles with monsters, and challenges from gods and goddesses, Joyce's novel takes place over a single day: June 16, 1904.

Medusa

Many poets from Shakespeare to Sylvia Plath have been inspired by Greek myth. The creative process of adapting these tales often provides the writers with an opportunity to explore themselves.

For example, Sylvia Plath was keen to explore matriarchal rage. She did so in her poem "Medusa" (1962). Its original title was "Mum: Medusa," and it looks at how her mother, her intimate familiar who nourished life, becomes a ghastly vision of death. The title itself suggests what a daughter is not permitted to say about her mother:

> Paralyzing the kicking lovers.
> Cobra light
> Squeezing the breath from the blood bells
> Of the fuchsia. I could draw no breath,
> Dead and moneyless.

Here, Plath evokes the threat of speech paralysis as a way of enforcing that silence. This example shows how modern genres often use the archetypes of Greek myth to explore themes salient to the present.

Influence of Greek Mythology on Art

A great deal of the understanding of classical mythology we have today comes from Renaissance art. During this period, much ancient wisdom was rediscovered, including Greek myth. Since then, Western art and artists have been inspired by these tales.

One early example is the 15th-century Italian artist Sandro Botticelli, who included mythological figures in many of his most popular works. He is known for his huge canvases, which incorporated images of mythical beings including Aphrodite in *The Birth of Venus* (ca. 1481–1486). Perhaps his most famous example is *La Primavera* (1477–1482), which is an allegorical representation of the spring (or *primavera* in Italian) depicting Aphrodite flanked by the Muses (Artsper, 2022).

Other artists influenced by Greek myth include the 16th-century artist Titian, who was commissioned by the Spanish court to create six paintings inspired by Ovid's *Metamorphoses* and other classical works. This took him the decade between 1551 and 1562 to complete. One example is *Danaë* (1554–1556), which tells the story of the daughter of King Acrisius of Argos. Her father shut her in a tower to prevent her from ever having a son who could succeed him as king.

These examples show how Greek mythology was often used in art to point the viewer toward cultural and social ideals or explore mythological themes and transmit them to a new audience.

Greek Mythology in Popular Culture Today: Reinterpretations and Retellings

Greek mythology continues to go through many reinterpretations and retellings, most recently through modern mediums such as film, television, comics, graphic novels, anime, and video games. Some of the most influential motifs that are still common in modern literature, poetry, and theater, such as epic journeys, transformation, revenge and power, and war and peace come from the canon.

Film

Two recent films that explore Greek myths are *Clash of the Titans* (1981, 2010) and *Troy* (2004). The former was originally released in 1981 and was remade in 2010. The film's plot is loosely based on the myth of the hero Perseus (see Chapter 2 for more details).

Troy, on the other hand, is loosely based on Homer's *Iliad* in its narration of the 10-year-long Trojan War. The film is a great introduction to the story, but it has also been reworked to make the narrative more appealing to a 21st-century audience. For this reason, it deviates from the original text in several key ways.

For one, there is the film's deviation in the depiction of the relationship between Achilles and Patroclus. In the movie, Achilles and Patroclus are portrayed as cousins, with Achilles (Brad Pitt) acting as a mentor to his younger relative. But ancient texts, including the *Iliad*, say that the two men were lovers. This adjustment makes sense when you consider the intensity of Achilles and Patroclus's fighting scenes and the warrior's anger and grief when Hector kills his companion. If the film had been made today, many producers wouldn't have shied away from depicting a gay relationship. But 2004 was a different time, and, back then, it was less acceptable to create a narrative where the main characters were in a same-sex romantic pairing.

The time span is another way in which the adaptation differs from Homer's original. While the film does not have a clear timeline, it is apparent that the events take place in a far shorter time than the original 10 years of the text. This makes sense in the context of a visual medium, as it means special effects aren't needed to age the actors, and it's easier for audiences to follow the action.

These examples show how modern depictions of ancient myths are often changed to make the narrative more appealing and relatable to a contemporary audience.

Video Games

Modern video games allow the player to explore the universe of Greek mythology for themselves, but they often deviate considerably from the source material.

God of War

The first era of the *God of War* video game franchise follows Kratos, a Spartan warrior, who becomes God of War and is in conflict with the Olympians. This era includes *God of War*, *God of War II*, *God of War: Betrayal*, *God of War: Chains of Olympus*, *God of War III*, *God of War: Ghost of Sparta*, and *God of War: Ascension*, all of which were released between 2005 and 2013.

Hades

Hades (2020) is a role-playing game where the main action takes place in the Greek underworld, from which it takes its name. The player controls Zagreus, the prince of this realm, who wants to escape from his unloving father and join his mother, Persephone, in the mortal realm.

The other Olympian gods support his quest and give him gifts (called "boons" in the game) to aid his fight against the beings that guard the exit to the underworld and prevent Zagreus from leaving. In his quest, he is also assisted by other residents of the realm such as Eurydice, Sisyphus, and Patroclus. The game involves four main dungeons: Asphodel, Tartarus, Elysium, and the Temple of Styx. Each of these represents one of the regions of Hades. Once one dungeon is cleared, the next is opened to the player.

Immortals Fenyx Rising

Immortals Fenyx Rising (2020) is narrated by Prometheus, who tells Zeus the story of Fenyx, a mortal who must rescue his brother by recapturing the evil Typhon after he escapes from the underworld.

The narrative director and lead writer of the game, Jeffrey Yohalem, was drawn to Greek myth for this game because he believes that these stories give contemporary audiences the kinds of heroes that appeal to them. He says (Burrows, 2020):

Right now, our heroes are being shown on camera all the time. We see them being selfish, we see them being clumsy falling down stairs, we see them making all kinds of mistakes. At the same time, everyone is under such pressure to curate their Instagram story to have the perfect relationship, the perfect food, and the perfect house, there's all this pressure to be perfect, but it's also increasingly impossible to be perfect. I feel like [Greek] mythology is the perfect lens to examine that.

In short, the imperfections of heroes and immortals that are so often emphasized in Greek myth make it the perfect genre to explore in the modern era, as it gives us imperfect characters that we can relate to.

Summary

In this chapter, we learned more about Greek mythology's legacy and how it continues to inspire modern works of fiction across diverse genres, including novels, poetry, video games, and films.

Moving on from this, we will sum up what we have learned in this book by presenting some conclusions on Greek mythology and its relevance to us today.

Chapter 12
CONCLUSION

Think not that your word and yours alone must be right.
— Sophocles, from Antigone

What We Have Learned

This book has covered all the key points of Greek mythology. We have learned all about the many gods and goddesses that the ancient Greeks worshiped, the love stories found in this canon, as well as its heroes and monsters, and its creation stories. We've also covered what it had to say about the afterlife and the underworld. Furthermore, we looked at the themes that occur and reoccur, such as transformation and metamorphosis, the myths' relationship to philosophy, and how they relate to other ancient mythologies and belief systems.

Another important point about Greek mythology that we explored is that it continues to influence us. It has informed the modern science of psychology and has shaped modern cultural output, from novels to video games.

All this tells us that Greek myths still matter today, even though we don't believe that they are true. This is not new: As early as the sixth century B.C.E., philosophers like the Stoics and Cynics were questioning the truth and validity of these tales. They concluded that the myths are allegories, not factual accounts. So, they offer us vital guidance on how to live our lives and tell us about the importance of certain qualities and values.

Lessons From the Ancient Greeks for Modern Life

Astonishingly, ancient Greece and its mythology are the source of much of our current culture and language. For example, many English words have roots in Greek mythology, like "tantalize" from Tantalus or "narcissism" from Narcissus, as well as many modern phrases and references. Some examples you might have heard are "Achilles' heel," meaning an individual weakness, or "Herculean task," meaning an impossible endeavor.

As the examples above suggest, many Greek myths were used to explain natural phenomena or human behavior. This is also exemplified by these stories being used to support theories proposed by early psychoanalysts such as Carl Jung and Sigmund Freud. One of the most famous of these cases is the Oedipus complex, named for the ancient tale of Oedipus, who killed his father and married his mother.

This shows that you can look for modern parallels in ancient narratives. Sylvia Plath did this in her poem "Medusa" when she compared the horror of the Gorgon to a hostile mother figure. Looking at interpretations of the same myth through different lenses can help us gain varied perspectives on it. A feminist perspective, like Plath's, may unleash new insights into Medusa and her monstrous appearance. Meanwhile, a psychoanalytical or Jungian standpoint can help us consider the motives behind the behavior of these mythical figures. Thus, there is no right or wrong way to interpret them.

Remember that since the time of the Stoics and Cynics, myths have been understood to represent deeper truths about human nature. That is why you should look for symbols and motifs in each story, such as the maze in the myth of Theseus and the Minotaur. Is that labyrinth a real, physical construction? Or, in actuality, is it symbolic of Theseus's inner journey and anxieties?

Above all, embrace the mystery! As in life, not all questions have clear answers in Greek mythology.

We hope you have enjoyed our brief introduction to Greek mythology. It is a highly complex and interesting subject, but we trust that what you have learned will inspire you to go on a journey to discover more.

If you have enjoyed reading this book, it would be greatly appreciated if you would take a moment to give it a quick review and rating on Amazon. This is so helpful in boosting its visibility.

To make this quick and easy for you, just scan the QR code of your country's marketplace to take you straight to the 'leave a review' section.

Many thanks again for choosing to read this book, and please keep your eye out for upcoming books in this series.

Neve.

www.nevesullivan.com

US: To leave a review on amazon.com:

Review link

UK: To leave a review on amazon.co.uk:

Review link

Australia: To leave a review on amazon.com.au:

Review link

Canada: To leave a review on amazon.ca:

Review link

OTHER BOOKS

A Beginner's Guide to Celtic Mythology: An Introduction to the Mysteries and Magic of Celtic Legend and Lore.

A Beginner's Guide to Celtic Spirituality: An Introduction to Celtic Spiritual Mysteries, Myths, and Rituals.

About the Author

Neve Sullivan's interest in ancient history and mythology is deeply rooted in her academic background and extensive travels around the world. She holds a BA Honors degree and a postgraduate diploma. Neve's dissertation focused on the cultural identity of Celtic lands, and in it she examined the Celts' unique expression through their literature, storytelling, poetry, song, and painting.

Neve's professional career in archives has led to a deep appreciation for historical texts and artifacts. She believes that understanding our historical roots enhances our appreciation for nature, brings magic into everyday life, and helps us value the arts as an integral part of our cultural identity.

Her books aim to help modern readers reconnect with ancient wisdom in a context that resonates with them, bridge gaps between past traditions and present realities, and remind us that there are timeless truths rooted in our history that still hold relevance today. Discover a new perspective on life and history with Neve Sullivan's series Ancient Wisdom for Modern Life and **Celtic Wisdom for Modern Life**.

For more about applying ancient wisdom to modern life, please visit: www.nevesullivan.com or scan the QR code below. As a thank you for signing up to my monthly newsletter, you will receive a free eBook as a gift, titled:

Guardians and Gatekeepers in Celtic Mythology.

Thank you for your interest in reading this book.

www.nevesullivan.com

REFERENCES & BIBLIOGRAPHY

Aeschylus. (2008). *Prometheus bound* (A. H. Sommerstein, Ed. and Trans.). Harvard University Press.

Allan, W. (2012). Divine justice and cosmic order in early Greek epic. *The Journal of Hellenic Studies*, 126. https://www.cambridge.org/core/journals/journal-of-hellenic-studies/article/abs/divine-justice-and-cosmic-order-in-early-greek-epic/CB65E5DCCDC3012ADCB581871BBC262F

Apuleius. (1822). *The Metamorphosis or Golden Ass, and philosophical works of Apuleius* (Thomas Taylor, Trans.). J. Moyes.

Artsper. (2022). How Botticelli's Three Graces changed art history. *Artsper Magazine*. https://blog.artsper.com/en/a-closer-look/how-botticellis-three-graces-changed-art-history/

Atlantic Religion. (2014). Similarities in Greco-Roman and Gaelic myth. https://atlanticreligion.com/2014/04/13/similarities-in-greco-roman-and-gaelic-myth/

Atwill, J. M. (1998). *Rhetoric reclaimed: Aristotle and the liberal arts tradition.* Cornell University Press.

Austin, N. (1990). *Meaning and being in myth.* The Pennsylvania State University Press.

Bane, T. (2020). *Encyclopedia of mythological objects*. McFarland & Company.

Beekes, R. S. P. (2009). *Etymological dictionary of Greek*. Brill.

Bell, R. E. (1991). *Women of classical mythology: A biographical dictionary*. Oxford University Press.

Bell, J. (2022). *Ancient philosophy as a way of living: Cynicism*. Classical Wisdom. https://classicalwisdom.com/philosophy/ancient-philosophy-as-a-way-of-living-cynicism-2/

Boardman, J. (1983). Atalanta. *Art Institute of Chicago Museum Studies*, 10: 3-19.

Borda, A. (2023). *Archetypes: Universal principles in myth and popular culture*. Pacifica News. https://www.pacifica.edu/pacifica-news/archetypes-universal-principles-in-myth-and-popular-culture/

Boulding, K. (2015). *Gastêr, Nêdys, and Thauma: Feminine sources of deception and generation in Hesiod's "Theogony."* [Master of Arts thesis, Dalhousie University Halifax, Nova Scotia].

Bravo, J. J. (2009). Recovering the past: The origins of Greek heroes and the hero cult. In S. Albersmeier (Ed.), *Heroes: Mortals and myths in ancient Greece*. Yale University Press.

Brown, C. S. (2014). *Greek origin story: The Titans and the gods of Olympus*. Khan Academy. https://www.khanacademy.org/humanities/big-history-project/what-is-big-history/origin-stories/a/origin-story-greek

Burrows, A. (2020). Interview: Jeffrey Yohalem discusses the myths and comedy that made Immortals Fenyx Rising. *The Sixth Axis*. https://www.thesixthaxis.com/2020/11/30/interview-jeffrey-yohalem-discusses-the-myths-and-comedy-that-made-immortals-fenyx-rising/

Burton, N. (2022). Plato's myths. *Philosophy Now.* https://philosophynow.org/issues/151/Platos_Myths

Buxton, R. (2009). *Forms of astonishment: Greek myth of metamorphosis.* Oxford University Press.

Camus, A. (1942). *The myth of Sisyphus.* Penguin.

Cartwright, M. (2012a, July 19). *Hades.* World History Encyclopedia. https://www.worldhistory.org/Hades/

Cartwright, M. (2012b, July 29). *Greek mythology.* World History Encyclopedia. https://www.worldhistory.org/Greek_Mythology/

Cartwright, M. (2015, July 27). *Pandora.* World History Encyclopedia. https://www.worldhistory.org/Pandora/

Cartwright, M. (2023, March 5). *Narcissus.* World History Encyclopedia. https://www.worldhistory.org/Narcissus/

Chaliakopoulos, A. (2021, February 1). *Top 13 stories of transformation in Greek mythology.* The Collector. https://www.thecollector.com/greek-mythology-stories-transformation/

Chaliakopoulos, A. (2024, February 14). *King Midas and his golden touch: A myth of riches & regret.* The Collector. https://www.thecollector.com/king-midas-golden-touch/

Clementi, E. (2009). *Greek myths and legends.* Lulu Press.

Colakis, M., & Masello, M. J. (2007). *Classical mythology & more: A reader workbook.* Bolchazy-Carducci Publishers, Inc.

Decherney, S. (2024, May 28). *Love.* Britannica. https://www.britannica.com/topic/love-emotion

Drabble, M. (Ed.). (1996). *The Oxford companion to English literature.* Oxford University Press.

The Editors of Encyclopedia Britannica. (2024a, January 19). *Morpheus*. Britannica. https://www.britannica.com/topic/Morpheus-Greek-mythology

The Editors of Encyclopedia Britannica. (2024b, February 13). *Oeneus*. Britannica. https://www.britannica.com/topic/Oeneus#ref968204

The Editors of Encyclopedia Britannica. (2024c, April 12). *Nymph*. Britannica. https://www.britannica.com/topic/nymph-Greek-mythology

The Editors of Encyclopedia Britannica. (2024d, April 16). *Ares*. Britannica. https://www.britannica.com/topic/Ares-Greek-mythology

The Editors of Encyclopedia Britannica. (2024e, April 25). *Midas*. Britannica. https://www.britannica.com/topic/Midas-Greek-mythology

The Editors of Encyclopedia Britannica. (2024f, April 30). *Ganymede*. Britannica. https://www.britannica.com/topic/Ganymede-Greek-mythology

The Editors of Encyclopedia Britannica. (2024g, May 27). *Aphrodite*. Britannica. https://www.britannica.com/topic/Aphrodite-Greek-mythology

The Editors of Encyclopedia Britannica. (2024h, May 28). *Pandora*. Britannica. https://www.britannica.com/topic/Pandora-Greek-mythology

The Editors of GreekMythology.com. (2024). *Birth of Athena*. GreekMythology.com https://www.greekmythology.com/Myths/The_Myths/Birth_of_Athena/birth_of_athena.html

Ellmann, R. (1972). *Ulysses on the Liffey*. Faber and Faber.

Estes, C. P. (1992). *Women who run with the wolves: Contacting the power of the wild woman*. Rider.

Fatica, M. (2021, September 24). *Who was the Greek goddess Hestia?* The Collector. https://www.thecollector.com/who-was-greek-goddess-hestia/

Felton, D. (2013). Rejecting and embracing the monstrous in ancient Greece and Rome. In A. S. Mittman & P. J. Dendle (Eds.), *The Ashgate research companion to monsters and the monstrous*. Routledge.

Ferguson, J. (2024, June 13). *Hellenistic age*. Britannica. https://www.britannica.com/event/Hellenistic-Age

The Fitzwilliam Museum. (2024). *The lyre*. University of Cambridge Museums & Botanic Garden. https://fitzmuseum.cam.ac.uk/explore-our-collection/highlights/context/sign-and-symbols/the-lyre

Foley, J. M. (1999). *Homer's traditional art*. Penn State Press.

Forbes Irving, P. M. C. (1990). *Metamorphosis in Greek myths*. Oxford University Press.

Gifford, D., & Seidman, R. J. (2008). *Ulysses annotated: Revised and expanded edition*. University of California Press.

Gish, D. A. (2023). *Xenophon's Socratic rhetoric: Virtue, Eros, and philosophy in the symposium*. Rowman & Littlefield.

Gleimius, N. (2022, February 1). *8 affairs of the Greek god Zeus*. The Collector. https://www.thecollector.com/affairs-greek-god-zeus/

Goddard, B. (2022). *Surfing the galactic highways: Adventures in divinatory astrology*. John Hunt Publishing.

Graf, F. (1993). *Greek mythology: An introduction*. John Hopkins University Press.

Grammarly. (2023, September 28). *The 12 steps of the hero's journey*. https://www.grammarly.com/blog/heros-journey/

Graves, R. (1955). *The Greek myths*. Penguin.

Greek Travel Tellers. (2020, October 31). *The Greek gods: Full list and background*. https://greektraveltellers.com/blog/the-greek-gods

Greeka. (n.d.). *Io and Zeus*. https://www.greeka.com/greece-myths/io-zeus/

Green, J. (2010). *Ancient Greek myths*. Gareth Stevens Publishing.

Green, P. (2023). *Another black book invoking*. Xlibris Corporation.

Grimal, P. (1996). *The dictionary of classical mythology*. Wiley-Blackwell.

Haase, C. (2007). *When Heimat meets Hollywood: German filmmakers and America, 1985–2005*. Camden House.

Hamilton, E. (2017). *Mythology: Timeless tales of gods and heroes*. Black Dog & Leventhal Publishers.

Hard, R. (2004). *The Routledge handbook of Greek mythology*. Routledge.

Hesiod. (1987). *Theogony* (S. Caldwell, Trans.). Hackett Publishing.

Hirschmann, K. (2012). *Medusa*. ReferencePoint Press, Inc.

History.com Editors. (2024, April 17). *Hercules*. History.com. https://www.history.com/topics/ancient-greece/hercules

Jung, C. G., & Kerenyi, K. (1963). *Essays on a science of mythology: The myth of the divine child and the mysteries of Eleusis*. Princeton University Press.

Kamlya, A. (2023, January 21). *Graces of Greek mythology: Origin, role, & significance*. Study.com. https://study.com/academy/lesson/graces-greek-mythology-origin-role.html

Kapach, A. (2023). *Titan Cronus*. Mythopedia. https://mythopedia.com/topics/cronus

Karoglou, K. (2018). *Dangerous beauty: Medusa in classical art*. Metropolitan Museum of Art.

Kerenyi, C. (1951). *The gods of the Greeks*. Thames & Hudson, Ltd.

Kingston, A. J. (2023). *Greek gods & goddesses: 4 in 1: Zeus, Hera, Poseidon, & Athena.* A. J. Kingston.

Kinsey, B. (2012). *Heroes and heroines of Greece and Rome.* Marshall Cavendish Corporation.

Knox, B. (1995). Introduction. In *The Odyssey* (R. Fagles, Trans.). Penguin Books.

Lancer, D. (2017, November 16). *Narcissus and Echo: The heartbreak of relationships with narcissists.* Codependency. https://whatiscodependency.com/relationships-with-narcissists-npd/

Lattimore, R. (Ed.). (1951). *The Iliad of Homer.* University of Chicago Press.

Lazzarus, L., & McCormick, C. (2024, June 13). *Homer or Hollywood: 5 inaccuracies in Brad Pitt's Troy (& 5 times they got it right).* Screen Rant. https://screenrant.com/troy-brad-pitt-movie-accurate-inaccurate/

Lesso, R. (2022a, May 18). *How did Perseus kill Medusa?* The Collector. https://www.thecollector.com/how-did-perseus-kill-medusa/

Lesso, R. (2022b, August 22). *Differences between ancient Greek and Roman gods? (15 deities).* The Collector. https://www.thecollector.com/what-are-the-differences-between-ancient-greek-and-roman-gods/

McGreevy, N. (2021, March 31). Why so many mythological monsters are female. *Smithsonian Magazine.* https://www.smithsonianmag.com/arts-culture/meet-female-monsters-greek-mythology-medusa-sphinx-180977364/

Mcleod, S. (2024, January 25). *Oedipus complex: Sigmund Freud mother theory.* Simply Psychology. https://www.simplypsychology.org/oedipal-complex.html#The-Electra-Complex

Mehrotra, M. (2016, August 14). *Greek and Norse mythology: A comparison*. The Avant Guardian. https://avantguardianblog.wordpress.com/2016/08/14/greek-and-norse-mythology-a-comparison/

Metcalf, C. (2015). *The gods rich in praise: Early Greek and Mesopotamian religious poetry*. Oxford University Press.

Monaghan, P. (1999). *The goddess path: Myths, invocations, & rituals*. Llewellyn Publications.

Morford, M. P. O., & Lenardon, R. J. (2003). *Classical mythology* (7th ed.). Oxford University Press.

The National Gallery. (2024). Titian's "poesie:" The commission. https://www.nationalgallery.org.uk/exhibitions/past/titian-love-desire-death/titian-s-poesie-the-commission

Noegel, S. B. (2006). Greek religion and the ancient Near East. In D. Ogden (Ed.), *The Blackwell companion to Greek religion*. Blackwell.

Obradovic, D. (2020). Filial estrangement and figurative mourning in the work of Nina Bunjevac. In M. Kuhlman & J. Alaniz (Eds.), *Comics of new Europe: Reflections and intersections*. Leuven University Press.

Ogden, D. (2001). *Greek and Roman necromancy*. Princeton University Press.

Padian, E. (2024, January 19). *Daedalus and Icarus: What is the main message?* The Collector. https://www.thecollector.com/daedalus-and-icarus-main-message/

Padman, R. (2023, August 12). *10 must-read ancient Greek tragedies*. The Collector. https://www.thecollector.com/ancient-greek-tragedies-must-read/

Park, A. (2014). Parthenogenesis in Hesiod's Theogony. *Preternature: Critical and Historical Studies on the Preternatural, 3*(2): 261–283.

Perera, A. (2024, February 13). *The Pygmalion effect: Definitions & examples*. Simply Psychology. https://www.simplypsychology.org/pygmalion-effect.html

Perseus Project. (2024). *Cerberus*. Perseus Digital Library. https://www.perseus.tufts.edu/Herakles/cerberus.html

Pollard, J. R. T., & Adkins, A. W. H. (2024). *Greek mythology*. Britannica. https://www.britannica.com/topic/Greek-mythology/Forms-of-myth-in-Greek-culture

Powell, B. B. (2007). *Classical myth* (5th ed.). Pearson/Prentice Hall.

Psychology Today Staff. (2024). *Projection*. Psychology Today. https://www.psychologytoday.com/gb/basics/projection

Puhvel, J. (1987). *Comparative mythology*. John Hopkins University Press.

Rae, H. (2010). *The mythology of Greek monsters*. Ragged University. https://raggeduniversity.co.uk/2012/11/03/mythology-greek-monsters-heather-rae/

Rattray, A. (2021, September 21). *Marcus Aurelius and Diogenes: Stoicism and cynicism*. Classical Wisdom. https://classicalwisdom.com/philosophy/marcus-aurelius-and-diogenes-stoicism-and-cynicism/

Reece, S. (2009). *Homer's winged words: The evolution of early Greek epic diction in the light of oral theory*. Brill.

Spicer, T. (2023). *Man-made: How the bias of the past is being built into the future*. Simon and Schuster.

Stapleton, M. (1986). *The illustrated dictionary of Greek and Roman mythology*. Peter Bedrick Books.

Stewart, I. (2011, February 17). *Echoes of Plato's Atlantis*. BBC History. https://www.bbc.co.uk/history/ancient/greeks/atlantis_01.shtml

Theoi Project. (n.d.-a). *Aphrodite loves 1*. https://www.theoi.com/Olympios/AphroditeLoves.html

Theoi Project. (n.d.-b). *Thanatos*. https://www.theoi.com/Daimon/Thanatos.html

Theoi Project. (n.d.-c). *Zeus loves 1*. https://www.theoi.com/Olympios/ZeusLoves.html

Unterrainer, H. F. (2023). On the trail of Sisyphus–Addiction as an existential neurosis? *Frontiers in Psychiatry*, 14. https://www.ncbi.nlm.nih.gov/pmc/articles/PMC10483396/

Van der Eijk, P. (2006). *Philoponus: On Aristotle on the soul 1.3-5*. Bloomsbury Academic.

Van Dyne, S. R. (1993). *Revising life: Sylvia Plath's Ariel poems*. The University of North Carolina Press.

Westmoreland, P. L. (2006). *Ancient Greek beliefs*. Lee and Vance Publishing Co.

White, D. A. (1993). *Rhetoric and reality in Plato's "Phaedrus."* State University of New York Press.

Wilkinson, P. (1998). *Illustrated dictionary of mythology: Heroes, heroines, gods, and goddesses from around the world*. Dorling Kingsley.

Williams, B. (2021, April 10). *The tragedy of Greek goddesses: Feminism in ancient Greece*. The Collector. https://www.thecollector.com/the-tragedy-of-greek-goddesses-feminism-in-ancient-greece/

Zimmerman, J. (2021). *Women and other monsters: Building a new mythology*. Beacon Press.